Looking *for* LOVE

Looking for LOVE

GEORGE BLOOMER

WHITAKER
HOUSE

**LOOKING FOR LOVE:
BUILDING RIGHT RELATIONSHIPS IN A
NOT-SO-RIGHT WORLD**
(Based on *When Loving You Is Wrong, But I Want To Be Right*, © 1997)

ISBN-13: 978-0-88368-991-2
ISBN-10: 0-88368-991-X
Printed in the United States of America
© 2004 by George G. Bloomer

Whitaker House
1030 Hunt Valley Circle
New Kensington, PA 15068
www.whitakerhouse.com

Library of Congress Cataloging-in-Publication Data

Bloomer, George G., 1963–
Looking for love / George Bloomer.
p.   cm.
ISBN 0-88368-991-X (trade pbk. : alk. paper)
1. Man-woman relationships—Religious aspects—Christianity. 2. Love—Religious aspects—Christianity. I. Title.
BT705.8.B55 2004
248.4—dc22
2004010768

---

2 3 4 5 6 7 8 9 10 11 12 ᵾ 12 11 10 09 08 07 06 05

Contents

Introduction

God has blessed me with the responsibility of delivering an essential message to the church concerning relationships, one of the most important areas of the natural lives of men and women throughout the world. I would like to share with you some of the many insights, revelations, and problem-solving truths He has caused me to recognize about this vital, but often little-understood, aspect of being human.

Somewhere, at some time, because of an intimate relationship, each of us was conceived in the flesh, birthed into sin, and enabled to become the functioning males and females we are today. We are all involved in relationships with other people. Although the number of established connections varies from person to person, none of us is an isolated hermit. In addition, relationships differ from one another in their degree of intimacy; familiarity can range from "just passing acquaintances" to "my one and only true love, my soul mate." Needless to say, acquaintanceships are much easier to make and maintain than very close connections.

Most people throughout the world at least acknowledge that a Supreme Being is the Maker of mankind. Almost all—saint and sinner alike—also admit that we need help and instruction in perfecting our personal, more intimate relationships. Where we seek that help, however, distinguishes the saint from the sinner. This particular book is addressed to and written for the edification of the church: those redeemed men and women everywhere who not only recognize, but also revere, the holy God as the one and only Creator of mankind; who have acknowledged their sinfulness and have offered repentance to His Son, Jesus, the one and only Savior of men's souls; who know Jesus as their personal Savior and Redeemer because He paid their sin-debt in full on the cross; and who, having given their hearts to God, also want to dedicate their minds and bodies, which are the vehicles for and the substance of their personal relationships.

Although the church is a spiritual entity, it is comprised of natural elements—flesh and blood, you and me—all trying to combine and unite together as the body of Christ. As flesh-and-blood human beings who are highly prone to error, we often operate our romantic relationships through our carnal natures. Doing so can create unhappy and unsuccessful situations, and our God-ordained service to others is negatively affected as a result.

While many Christians do abide in healthy, positive, productive relationships, many of us—perhaps too many of us—do not. As it now stands, members of the church are spotted with the plague of forbidden relationships: those person-to-person, body-to-body, and soul-to-soul unions that are not sanctioned by God. Such unions are the intimate and potentially intimate relations between consenting adults that simply do not bear the Lord's seal of approval.

Forbidden relationships are found in the majority of the unfruitful, unsaved lives of the earth's men and women. They should not, however, mark Christ's church. The evidence that they do is found in the abundance of problem-ridden unions and troubled marriages, as well as the open display of unconfessed sexual sins within circles of God's people. By being able to know and recognize the symptoms and signposts of forbidden relationships in our midst, we can help prevent the sin and fatal consequences of individuals' unrighteous living from affecting and infecting the collective body of Christ.

If the truth were told, most of us have experienced the pain and suffering of at least one bad relationship at one time or another in our lives. Notwithstanding, the liberating truth is that wholesome, strong, and fruitful unions can and will be ours when we learn to attract godly people into our lives. This only happens as we follow the guidelines of the infallible Word of God.

Even if God has graced you with a healthy, committed relationship, this book is still for you. Read on, and allow it to make you aware of the biblical origins of bad relationships, what God's Word says concerning these relationships, what it is that makes your own union successful, and how you can help others to be as blessed as you are.

God is the only perfect being, and we know that we, with our sinful natures, will not achieve perfection on earth in any relationship. However, this is no excuse not to strive for better, more harmonious relations with our fellowmen—and especially those fellowmen we call boyfriend, girlfriend, partner, spouse, mate, and fiancé(e).

Read and learn to follow God's prescription for relationships.

—George G. Bloomer

Part I

The Amazing Maze Called Love

1

Why We Love to Love, and Why It's So Hard

Chapter One

Why We Love to Love, and Why It's So Hard

Whether you're married, divorced, dating often, or not dating at all, I think you'll agree that relationships are not easy. It seems that each person has more than he or she can handle in navigating this crazy life without throwing another person into the mix, especially a person with whom you're supposed to "be one." How are you supposed to preserve your individuality and yet support, love, and become one with someone else? And where is this special someone to be found anyway?

Despite the numerous complications a committed relationship entails, we all long to have that special kind of union with another human being in which we truly know and are known by each other. We desire that this knowledge be intimate, perceptive, total, and complete—a deep heart knowledge. We desperately want to be accepted, loved, and cherished for who we really are, in spite of our flaws and imperfections. Built into the human condition is a longing not to have to play games by pretending to be someone we are not; we want to be able to be authentic with at least one other person and still be loved. Moreover, we want our Mr. and Ms. Rights to be our perfect counterparts, loving and accepting us unselfishly and eternally.

The need for intimacy is woven into the fabric of our lives; we can't make it disappear by praying it away, by willing it to leave, or by ignoring it.

That concept, with slight personal variations, is the image of the ideal relationship we each carry deep inside. Why do we desire it? Because God has designed us to be relational beings. The need for intimacy is woven into the fabric of our lives; we can't make it disappear by praying it away or by willing it to leave or by ignoring it. Each of us must come to terms with this aspect of life and with how to meet this burning desire for relational fulfillment legitimately, no matter what our marital status may be.

That being said, let me remind you that it is not easy. But, then again, no one ever said it would be. After all, the first committed relationship ever (Adam and Eve's) took a nosedive that has caused every generation to be born into sin, incapable of pure love.

Who Said It Would Be Easy?

As we delve into this timely topic, let us take a look at the very first record the Bible gives of a relationship deemed unacceptable in the eyes of God—a relationship with sin. Although this first forbidden relationship took place thousands of years ago, it still has repercussions for us today.

> *Now the serpent was more cunning than any beast of the field which the LORD God had made. And he said to the woman, "Has God indeed said, 'You shall not eat of every tree of the garden'?" And the woman said to the serpent, "We may eat the fruit of the trees of the garden; but of the fruit of the tree which is in the midst of the garden, God has said, 'You shall not eat it, nor shall you touch it, lest you die.'" Then the serpent said to the woman, "You will not surely die. For God knows that in the day you eat of it your eyes will be opened, and you will be like God, knowing good and evil." So when the woman saw that the tree was good for food, that it was pleasant to the eyes, and a tree desirable to make one wise, she took of its fruit and ate. She also gave to her husband with her, and he ate.* (Genesis 3:1–6)

We find in Genesis that the very first sin was the one Adam and Eve committed when they both ate of the forbidden fruit from the Tree of the Knowledge of Good and Evil. We all know the story, many of us having learned it as children in Sunday school. But, when reading this passage, how often do we consider that Adam and Eve's sin began sometime before Eve took that first bitter bite and Adam thoughtlessly followed her sinful lead?

In the first verse of the text, we read, *"And* [the Serpent] *said to the woman,"* and in the second verse, *"And the woman said to the serpent."* Here in this initial verbal exchange, the discerning spiritual eye can see a catastrophe about to take place. Eve, the mother of humanity, had begun at this very point to enter into a definite, certain relationship with sin. How? By merely conversing with the Serpent!

Where was Adam while all this conversing was taking place? Why didn't he warn Eve not to engage in conversation with Satan, not to flirt with temptation? He was not there to provide wise counsel or to prevent her from speaking with the Serpent, though it is doubtful that he would have been much help if he had been there. After all, Eve didn't need to do much convincing to get him to eat some of the tempting fruit as well.

And so, through the bait of conversation, Satan convinced Eve, and thus Adam, to bite into the forbidden fruit. Before we examine exactly how it was that the woman partook of the fruit, let us first determine why it was that Eve even took a chance on exchanging pleasantries with the Devil in the first place.

In the beginning of our text, we read, *"Now the serpent was more subtle than any beast of the field which the LORD God had made"* (Genesis 3:1 KJV). The word *"subtle"* is defined by *Webster's New Collegiate Dictionary* as "highly skillful, artful, crafty, difficult to understand or distinguish, obscure, crafty, highly skillful, operating insidiously." Certainly, we Christians know Satan to be all of these things—skillfully clever, crafty, sly, insidious, hard to detect, and so on.

On Satan's first day of business with this new creature, Man—and more precisely, Woman—he was, no doubt, on his best demonic behavior! With the very same tactics he employs today to tempt and trick God's people, the Enemy set out to ruin Eve. As a maneuvering serpent, he was slick, seductive, quick-witted, smooth-talking, cunning, and quietly aggressive. But, more than any of his outer charms, Satan used conversation as a weapon against Eve. He smooth-talked her into communicating with him, questioning God, influencing Adam to sin, and, ultimately, disobeying God.

For God knows that in the day you eat of it your eyes will be opened, and you will be like God, knowing good and evil. So when the woman saw that the tree was good for food, that it was pleasant to the eyes, and a tree desirable to make one wise, she took of its fruit and ate. She also gave to her husband with her, and he ate.
(Genesis 3:5–6)

And the result was that every person from then until the Judgment Day has been and will be born with sin. It is in our nature to disobey and reject God. And if it is so much a part of our natures to be at odds with our loving Creator, how much more is it a part of our natures to confuse and upset our relationships with other humans?

It is in our nature to disobey and reject God.

Relationships are difficult and sometimes destructive because that is human nature. Because of Adam and Eve's first relationship with sin, every relationship that followed was tainted, this includes ours today. Stemming out of that one error is all our imperfect love. All our self-love and pride can be traced back to our first representatives on earth and the tragic decision they made.

We're Not Improving Things

That isn't the end of the story though. Society today continues to degrade and deteriorate when it comes to romantic attachments. Adam and Eve left the garden, yes, but they left in a committed, God-sanctioned relationship. Today, that type of relationship is hard to come by. Homosexuality, fornication, and adultery run rampant and confuse the true meaning of relationships even further.

God gave the gift of sexuality for the purpose of pleasure and reproduction within the covenant bonds of marriage. Satan, however, has sought to distort the purity of such a bond and to destroy lives by warping and perverting the work of God. Just look at all of the news stories today regarding great leaders involved in perverse or immoral sexual acts. Read the statistics about teen pregnancy and abortion. Look around and see how many marriages end in divorce. All this was obviously not God's original intention, but our perversion of His perfect provision for us.

God's Intention versus Our Perversion

God desires that the strongest and most intimate relationship any of His children have with another human being be the marriage union. Because He designed marriage as the foundation for all other societal structures, the marital unit needs to have the most strength so that it can stand up under the negative pressures and forces of this world.

To help form and fortify the bond between a husband and a wife, and thus strengthen their marriage, God created the most effective glue known—sexual intimacy. Sex was designed by God not just as the means of producing offspring, but more basically as the bonding agent to unite two individuals together on all levels—body-to-body, soul-to-soul, and spirit-to-spirit.

Therefore a man shall leave his father and mother and be joined to his wife, and they shall become one flesh.
(Genesis 2:24)

God designed sex to be very pleasurable physically and emotionally so that it would have an addictive quality to it. The better a behavior makes us feel, the more we repeat it; so the more a couple engages in the delights and pleasures of sexual intimacy, the more the soul tie between them is intensified and the stronger the marriage bond becomes. Because sexual intimacy exponentially reinforces the soul-tie bonds between the partners, sexual relations are to be kept strictly within the confines of the marriage union.

Marriage is honorable among all, and the bed undefiled; but fornicators and adulterers God will judge.
(Hebrews 13:4)

God isn't the cruel Judge that some think He is. After all, He is the Designer of our sexuality in the first place. He just designated boundaries—for our good.

As commanded by God in His Word, sex outside of marriage is illegal, and breaking this law can have phenomenal repercussions. Sexual involvement can form such an entangling web of soul ties that certain relationships became nearly impossible to break away from. Like powerful, mature tree roots, multiple soul ties can often reach deep into an individual's personality and spirit, becoming a part of his or her very being.

God isn't the cruel Judge that some think He is. He just designated boundaries—for our good.

Furthermore, when a person engages in promiscuous sex, the soul of the practicing individual is divided and subsequently scattered among his or her multiple partners. This may appear to be especially true where women are concerned, because soul ties are so emotionally binding and women are particularly susceptible in the area of emotions. Thus, women have trouble severing the emotional cords to their sexual partners and will often attempt to reestablish the emotional bonds, no matter how detrimental they may be. The Bible declares that men are just as bound to their previous sex partners, even though it might not be as readily apparent since men tend not to exhibit the emotionalism women do about the breakup of an affair.

> Do you not know that he who is joined to a harlot is one
> body with her? For "the two," He says, "shall become
> one flesh." (1 Corinthians 6:16)

Men are often so strongly tied to their prior liaisons in their visual and physical memories that they will habitually try to repeat the sexual encounters.

Frequently, the souls of people who have been promiscuous in sex are drawn to those of all their previous partners, even long after the relationships have ended. This can happen to such an extent that when these people marry, they often develop sexual and communication problems with their mates.

Undoing the Knot

After the knitting together of souls in an illegal rendezvous has taken place, a spiritual untying is required for deliverance. The Word of God tells us that we have the power both to bind and to loose.

> *And I will give you the keys of the kingdom of heaven, and whatever you bind on earth will be bound in heaven, and whatever you loose on earth will be loosed in heaven.* (Matthew 16:19)

It is of great importance that we loose every knot that has been illegally tied in our lives. The knitting together of two souls within a marriage can bring forth good fruit. However, any illicit ties or knots need to be broken. Pray the following prayer and believe in your heart that it will result in your being loosed from the snare of the soul tie.

> Heavenly Father,
> In the name of Jesus, I submit all of my soul, my body, my desires, and my emotions to You and Your Spirit. I denounce any conscious or subconscious attachments formed in my past: past involvements, past emotional attachments, and past premarital sexual relationships. I denounce the emotional, physical, and spiritual ties formed by my involvement in any forbidden sexual, mental, or emotional intimacy outside of my marriage. I confess all of my ungodly spirit, soul, and body ties

as sin. I thank You for forgiving me and cleansing me of all unrighteousness, right now!

I loose myself from all soul ties to past sexual partners and ungodly relationships. Please uproot all connections through sexual bondage, sexual deviations, emotional longings, dependencies, perversions, and enslaving thoughts and fantasies. I bind every evil spirit that reinforced the soul tie and any evil transference into my life through ungodly associations.

Lord, I ask You to cleanse my soul and to erase totally from my memory bank all illicit unions that I participated in. Set me free so that I may serve only the purposes of God and my mate.

Father, now that I have asked You this and know it is in accordance with Your will for my life, I believe I am totally forgiven and set free. I recommit myself to You and my mate, in Jesus' name. Amen

If you prayed this prayer with genuineness and sincerity, you are now starting a clean slate with God and your spouse or spouse-to-be. Get ready for an explosively wonderful relationship.

Defining a True Relationship

Most of us define a true relationship in terms of knowing and being known, accepting and being accepted, loving and being loved, while often emphasizing such additional components as commitment, communication, romance, and chemistry. Yet, in our attempts to find and establish our dream friendships and unions, we have taken forbidden, fruitless sidetracks that lead to dead ends instead of staying on the path that *"leads to life"* (Matthew 7:14), the path that God has specifically planned for each one of us.

Often, we have gone off in the opposite direction from the way God wants us to travel as we try to fill the aching void in our hearts through a relationship with another person. We have searched for the missing pieces of our souls in other imperfect, flawed individuals, who generally respond to us from positions of neediness as well. We have failed to heed God's map and the directions He has carefully written out for us to follow. He has told us exactly where we can find our wholeness and how our desires can be met:

> *Delight yourself also in the LORD, and He shall give you the desires of your heart. Commit your way to the LORD, trust also in Him, and He shall bring it to pass.*
>
> (Psalm 37:4–5)

> *But seek first the kingdom of God and His righteousness, and all these things shall be added to you.*
>
> (Matthew 6:33)

When the Spirit of the Lord draws two people together, you can be assured that the relationship will be "a match made in heaven."

Most of us define a true relationship in terms of knowing and being known, accepting and being accepted, loving and being loved.

Read on to discover God's starting point for your journey toward fulfilling relationships. As you learn to build and foster the relationships in your life so that they develop into fabulous ones, may God smile upon you in His infinite love and transform your world in His righteousness.

Relationships: The Way They Work

Chapter Two

Relationships: The Way They Work

God gave us a fundamental principle for the management of our lives when He said, *"Let all things be done decently and in order"* (1 Corinthians 14:40). This general pattern is applicable not only in the use of His gifts and the conduct of worship services but also in the development of healthy, fulfilling relationships.

Our Lord has shown us where to begin as we aim for true intimacy with another person. In order for us to establish a solid foundation on which to build an unshakable union, we believers need to proceed as follows:

1. We need to develop an intimate, personal relationship with God.

2. Before becoming involved with another person, we must first get to know ourselves—who we are as individuals and who we are in Christ.

3. If we are to love and accept another person, we must first learn to love and accept ourselves.

The more we grow to love and depend upon the Lord, the more He reveals to us just who we are in Him, thereby enabling us to love ourselves. And the better we know, love, and appreciate who we are, the better prepared we are to extend these same feelings and sentiments to our loved ones.

Inestimable Value

True self-esteem does not come from achievements or material possessions, and it cannot be found in human relationships. If it could, would people who are financially bankrupt, unemployed, or divorced have no value? Of course not! Our real worth is derived from a close, personal relationship with God and from who we are in Christ.

As we believers spend time in the presence of the Lord, we allow Him to sanctify us by washing us with the cleansing water of His Word (Ephesians 5:26) and to pour out His love upon us. When the realization hits us that Christ loved us so much that He endured the agonies of crucifixion in order to redeem us from eternal death, we will come to know how truly valuable we are. He bought us with His life! That gives each of us an inestimable value.

> The more we grow to love and depend upon the Lord, the more He reveals to us just who we are in Him, thereby enabling us to love ourselves.

Thus, we do not have to find our worth in another person's opinion of us or in how much "stuff" we own or in what we do—even if what we do is for the Lord. Because our value is rooted and grounded in Christ, we can then enter into relationships with others, not out of desperate neediness, but out of a desire to share and to enrich our lives.

Developing Relational Skills: My Story

The art of relationships cannot be taught. We must learn through trial and error in order to develop our own abilities to interrelate. I believe that, to a large extent, we are products of our environments, where most of life's lessons are *caught* instead of *taught*. From the role models around us, we pick up our views about living, especially on how to relate to others.

Such was the case in my life. I grew up in a large family of nine children. Because my father was absent most of the time, our mother was stretched to her limits trying to raise us. She had little or no reserves from which to teach us how to live and love. Survival was the goal in our family. Thus, I found myself looking for love in all the wrong places. I went from one relationship to the next. Each began very quickly and ended just as abruptly.

Even after I was born again and had come into the church, the area of male/female relationships was still distorted for me. Finding myself constantly looking for the right relationship, I invested a lot of time going to movies, ball games, and other events where I thought I could meet the "right" woman for me. Unfortunately, I was involved in a lot of activities that I really did not enjoy, just so I could continue to meet up with young ladies who were not compatible with me.

Furthermore, at that time the church had no real training for someone like me in how to live as a godly man or how to act as a gentleman. Since I had come from the streets, I needed to be mentored in how to conduct myself generally and relationally. I had seen my mother being abused and just assumed that this was the way men treated women. Since my dad abused my mother, I erroneously thought that if a man was going to have a good relationship, he had to put the woman "in check" by taking control and exerting authority over her.

I Met a Man

Because of my upbringing, by the time I reached the age of seventeen, I was an out-of-control, unsaved young man on my way to prison. Accompanying me into that tiny cell in Rikers Island was my two-hundred-dollar-a-day cocaine habit. There, cornered in that little cell where I could not run and hide, I met Jesus. Later, I would be able to say, along with the woman at the well, *"Come, see a Man who told me all things that I ever did"* (John 4:29). Jesus knew all about me and my past, yet He still loved me and wanted me.

However, it was not until He got me backed up against the wall that I said yes to Him. I thought that saying yes to the Lord was going to get me out of my predicament. Little did I know that saying yes to Him was saying yes to a number of things: yes to His will, yes to His ways, yes to His becoming the Ruler, Governor, and Leader of my life.

Surprisingly, I also found that the Man I vaguely remembered hearing about in Sunday school was really a person, a person who could touch me, with arms that could embrace and hold me. His voice would guide and correct me. He blessed me, but He also chastised me.

I discovered the true meaning of love from this Man who provided all the things that I had needed from a natural father but had never received. Needless to say, I was thrilled that there was finally a Man—a male role model and father figure all combined into one—in my life. I had tapped into the ultimate relationship. I loved Jesus, and He loved me.

New Man, New Relationships

Out of this relationship with my Lord and Savior, I began to develop a deep concern for other people. I became compassionate and very sensitive to the needs and hurts of others. I had never really experienced these feelings before. I entered into a discipline through which new qualities and a new character started to form within me. I began to live and act differently from the old me.

Therefore, if anyone is in Christ, he is a new creation;
old things have passed away; behold, all things have
become new. (2 Corinthians 5:17)

In truth, through my relationship with Jesus Christ, I was transformed into a brand-new person. Up to that point, all the relationships I had been involved in (and had eventually lost) had been a waste of time, because I had not known who I was. When I realized who I was in Christ, I quickly discovered the type of people who would be right for me, based upon the new person I had become through my relationship with Christ.

As I grew closer to my Savior, I learned a number of things about myself and about relationships. First was the fact that there were individuals to whom I was very attracted but who were dangerous for me to associate with. Thus, I had to learn the discipline of distancing myself from people who could be a bad influence on me. Their enticements could have been very detrimental to my walk with the Lord, so I could not allow them to get close.

We tend to want to rush ahead of God's timing, believing that we have become mature enough to handle an intimate union.

Even through the long, difficult process of relearning how to relate to others God's way, I found companionship in my relationship with Jesus Christ. As He showed me who He was, I in turn opened myself up to Him and finally admitted to Him who I had been and who I was becoming.

Waiting for a Supernatural Introduction

Only after I had found out who I was in Christ could I truly embrace another individual and allow her to become an intimate part of my life. It is not until believers find contentment in their fellowship with the Lord that they can truly experience the joys of close human relationships.

However, we need to wait on God to introduce us to His choice of the right mate for us. We tend to want to rush ahead of God's timing, believing that we have become mature enough to handle an intimate union. We often choose a mate hurriedly and therefore unwisely. Because we fail to take the time to know ourselves and to discipline our lower passions by not permitting these desires to take precedence over our spirits, we often find ourselves in a quagmire of marital confusion and disharmony.

Only God can transform that mismatched, ill-advised relationship into something of beauty and unity. But, thank God, He is more than able to take our mistakes, as we surrender them, and to use them for our good. If He can change us from sinners into saints, He is quite capable of transforming our bad relationships into good ones.

Now to Him who is able to do exceedingly abundantly above all that we ask or think, according to the power that works in us. (Ephesians 3:20)

For with God nothing will be impossible. (Luke 1:37)

And we know that all things work together for good to those who love God, to those who are the called according to His purpose. (Romans 8:28)

The Trust Factor

When two people are being knit together in intimate union, the process often seems a bit overwhelming, yet pleasurable at the same time. When the two enter into each other's secret closets, they can sometimes exit shocked at the unexpected things they found there. It is wise to proceed with caution, because emotions can be highly sensitive as souls are bared by both partners. Not since the garden of Eden has it been easy for any of us to reveal our innermost selves to another person.

> *And they were both naked, the man and his wife, and were not ashamed.* (Genesis 2:25)

This process of bonding occurs as we allow ourselves to be vulnerable with our mates and learn to trust their responses to our self-disclosures. However, we can easily violate our spouses' trust and destroy those newly formed bonds when we react to their revelations with suspicious accusations. Additionally, the couple must not only trust each other, but most importantly trust God.

> *Blessed is that man who makes the LORD his trust.* (Psalm 40:4)

But what does one do when the marital trust has been broken? My marriage had to stand the test of trust: I was accused of having extramarital tendencies, not with another woman, but with my ministry. I was heavily engrossed in the problems of other individuals in my church, and I mistakenly took for granted the security of my marriage, neglecting to use proper caution. Although all the material needs of my wife and family were being met, I was failing to meet their emotional needs.

Outside In; Inside Out

Men tend to operate from the outside in, while women tend to function from the inside out. Men deal with life on the surface by meeting the everyday material needs of the family and maintaining a certain standard of external structure in the household. A woman's creativity, however, comes from within. While the bills must be paid and the home kept in an orderly fashion for a wife to feel secure, this must be accompanied by emotional, mental, and spiritual support from her spouse so that she can fully develop her potential. When a husband breaks his promise to be all these things for his wife, her trust in the marriage and in her husband is also broken.

This process of bonding occurs as we risk being vulnerable with our mates and learn to trust their responses to our self-disclosures.

So, what do you do when the bond of trust in a relationship has been betrayed and violated? The answer in my case was simply, "It took God." God used my wife to point out to me my neglect of the marriage, of her, and surprisingly, of God as well. I was so busy doing the *work* of God that I had gotten out of the *will* of God.

While mending what had been torn, I discovered that, in addition to repenting to God, there were also some things that I had to do for myself. No longer could I attend to others and their problems when mine were not being addressed. I had to take the time to reestablish and renew my personal relationship with God. I immediately began to fellowship with Him on a regular basis. I ministered unto Him, and He ministered back to me. I entered into a season of weeping, worship, and divine fellowship with God, in which He became the love of my soul and my life.

I found that as I consistently sought the Lord, the things that were most lacking in me and in my marriage were restored one by one in their fullness. I was reacquainted with my wife and she with me. God's miraculous power of bonding two people together in love united us once again as *"one flesh"* (Matthew 19:6) in His sight. This bond is even stronger now than it was then.

Ministry Is No Excuse

Some people may argue that as long as a man is doing the work of the Lord, his wife should understand and not complain. However, 1 Timothy 5:8 states, *"But if anyone does not provide for his own, and especially for those of his household, he has denied the faith and is worse than an unbeliever."* In this case, the word *"provide"* is not to be interpreted as having only a financial connotation, although that is very pertinent. Here, *"provide"* means supplying the godly support necessary in order to sustain a well-equipped marriage and family, even through the trials and tests of life. Ministers of the Gospel are first responsible for the well-being of their own families.

Traveling Companions

Often a couple must endure hardships together in order to keep the blessing and promises of God within the marriage. This reality is illustrated by the story of Abraham and

Sarah in Genesis. Their marriage was ordained by God, who promised to bless them not only individually but collectively as well. Throughout their many tests and trials, Abraham and Sarah remained faithful to each other. An important factor is that Sarah and Abraham each had a personal relationship with God. Both of them had their faith invested in God and in His ability to bring His words to pass. At different times Sarah and Abraham had to individually depend on God to meet their needs, instead of looking to one another for the fulfillment of their expectations. Because of this, the blessings of God rested on their marriage and even continued down to their offspring. We must understand that although a couple can praise God and pray together, worship, faith, and a divine relationship with God are very personal.

Therefore know that the LORD your God, He is God, the faithful God who keeps covenant and mercy for a thousand generations with those who love Him and keep His commandments. (Deuteronomy 7:9)

God's Plan for You

"For I know the plans that I have for you," declares the LORD, "plans for welfare and not for calamity to give you a future and a hope." (Jeremiah 29:11 NAS)

Discover the plan of God for your own personal life before bringing someone else into it with you. In order to love your mate as God has ordained and purposed in His Word, you must first love God and then love yourself.

So husbands ought to love their own wives as their own bodies; he who loves his wife loves himself. (Ephesians 5:28)

Marriage is honorable in the sight of God, and both mates should treat this sacred union and their partner with admiration, love, and respect. Putting God first in every endeavor and with each fascinating step in the process of bonding together will help to keep God's blessing on your relationships. "It took God" for me and my marriage, and surely it will take God for yours, whether you have found your mate yet or not.

3

Are You in the Right Place?

Chapter Three

Are You in the Right Place?

met him at the supermarket when I accidentally walked straight into him with my arms full of groceries. He helped me clean up the mess, and the rest is history."

"We went to high school together, but I hadn't seen her in years. Then, we bump into each other one night on the other side of the country. Go figure!"

Do either of these scenarios sound familiar? It seems like there are a lot of "right place at the right time" stories out there. Stories where "fated" and unexpected encounters lead to a lifetime of love together. You have to admit the thought is alluring. At any moment you could turn a corner and run into the man or woman of your dreams. One minute, single and alone; the next, swept up in a beautiful romance.

Then again, realistically speaking, these stories are not the norm. Most romances are a lot less spontaneous and a lot more run-of-the-mill: Boy meets girl, boy likes girl, girl likes boy, the wedding bells ring. Furthermore, even when a romance springs from a unique chance encounter, it's not "we met, we loved one another, we lived happily ever after." Nope, even those whom fate brought together in aisle number seven of their local supermarket still have to deal with the mundane, and sometimes volatile, ups and downs of dating, engagement, and marriage.

But, I don't want to completely rain on your parade. There still is a lot to be said for being in the right place at the right time. That's not to say you should wear your favorite dress shirt or put on that new skirt just to go to the super-market—you know, just in case. What I mean is that you need to be in a position to find lasting love. Where is this magic "position"? Right behind God, following Him toward His will for your life.

Please, God, Not a Zebra!

And the LORD God formed man of the dust of the ground, and breathed into his nostrils the breath of life; and man became a living being. The LORD God planted a garden eastward in Eden, and there He put the man whom He had formed....Then the LORD God took the man and put him in the garden of Eden to tend and keep it.
(Genesis 2:7–8, 15)

God made Adam and gave him a purpose—to tend and keep the garden. But God realized that Adam was alone and needed a helper. He needed a female counterpart.

> And the LORD God said, "It is not good that man should be alone; I will make him a helper comparable to him." Out of the ground the LORD God formed every beast of the field and every bird of the air, and brought them to Adam to see what he would call them. And whatever Adam called each living creature, that was its name. So Adam gave names to all cattle, to the birds of the air, and to every beast of the field. But for Adam there was not found a helper comparable to him. And the LORD God caused a deep sleep to fall on Adam, and he slept; and He took one of his ribs, and closed up the flesh in its place. Then the rib which the LORD God had taken from man He made into a woman, and He brought her to the man. (Genesis 2:18–22)

God knew Adam needed a suitable mate. And God had a plan to provide that mate for Adam. But did God just make Eve and hand her over, saying, "Here you go, Adam. She's the one for you"? No, Adam had to look first. Adam had to follow God's plan, exercising his dominion over creation as he named each of the animals and found none of them to be suitable as a mate.

Don't commit the rest of your life to something you know won't bless you.

God knew that a zebra wasn't going to cut it for Adam. He knew that Adam needed Eve. But He allowed Adam to find that out for himself and to do a little of God's work (naming the animals and caring for the garden) before He created Eve. Essentially, God said, "Adam, I know you need a helper. You need a wife. You need someone to help you do what I've called you to do. But I don't just want to hand her to you. I want you to look through all My other creation, naming them and not finding any of them suitable. Then, when I give you Eve, you will truly recognize how perfect she is for you."

It's a good thing Adam was in his correct position, following God's will for his life. What if Adam had gotten a little desperate at the last moment and opted to take a hyena as his bride? That certainly would have put a whole new twist on our world today. But he didn't. Adam would not commit the rest of his life to something he knew couldn't bless him. He looked and, just like God, he recognized that his suitable mate was not among the animals he saw before him in the garden.

Similarly, we need to do our bit of looking. We need to look through a few zebras and elephants before we find the right one for us. Because, otherwise, how will we recognize the right one? In the following chapters we're going to look at some unsuitable relationships for the purpose of finding out what a suitable one is. But right now, let's look at Adam's response to God's newest creation—Eve.

And Adam said: "This is now bone of my bones and flesh of my flesh; she shall be called Woman, because she was taken out of Man." Therefore a man shall leave his father and mother and be joined to his wife, and they shall become one flesh. (Genesis 2:23–24)

Adam saw Eve and connected with her. He saw her and recognized his rib—that missing part of him. He said, "This is the one. This is my rib. She's already part of me."

Are you following God's will for your relationships? Are you in the place you should be or are you hanging out with the zebras and hyenas, hoping something will happen or forcing an unhealthy relationship? Examine your walk with God as you read this book and see whether you're in the position to receive your perfect mate from God.

Wrong Place at the Wrong Time

Of course, if it's possible to be in the right place to pursue lasting love, it's also possible to be in the wrong place.

The story of King David's greatest sin is also the Bible's classic tale of adultery. Concerning desire, lust, love, faithfulness, service, deceit, and murder, the soap-opera-style love triangle of David, Bathsheba, and Uriah quite obviously provides many moral lessons about adultery, murder, and disobedience. However, underneath the obvious morals of this fascinating story lies a most profound principle to be discovered: A person's location in life often determines his position in life.

> It happened in the spring of the year, at the time when kings go out to battle, that David sent Joab and his servants with him, and all Israel; and they destroyed the people of Ammon and besieged Rabbah. But David remained at Jerusalem.　　　　　(2 Samuel 11:1)

This first verse reveals to us that Israel's greatest and most beloved leader, King David, was—as are all people at some time or another in their lives—out of position, because he was in the wrong place at the wrong time. How do we know this? The Scripture informs us that *"at the time when kings go out to battle...David remained at Jerusalem."* In biblical times, war would sometimes break out in different areas, and the king was expected to act as the military commander in chief. Presumably, everyone in the region knew war had come. So, all of the region's kings acted accordingly, fulfilling the expectation and requirement that they go off and protect their territories through war. One king, however, stayed behind.

A person's location in life often determines his position in life.

David himself was obviously very conscious that it was time for war, for he sent Joab and his servants to war on Israel's behalf. But somehow, David failed to look down at his own two feet and command them to carry him to the battlefield! Instead, according to this passage, he *"remained at Jerusalem."* He did not go when and where his kingly position dictated he ought to go.

> *Then it happened one evening that David arose from his bed and walked on the roof of the king's house. And from the roof he saw a woman bathing, and the woman was very beautiful to behold.* (2 Samuel 11:2)

Scripture tells us that David awoke from a late afternoon nap and walked out onto his rooftop. I imagine that, because he was the king, David's palace sat higher than everyone else's, making it possible for him to overlook all of the surrounding buildings. So, he would frequently come out on his flat roof to survey the city. However, on this particular visit to the top of his palace, David paused for more than just a glance over the local region. He got an eyeful of a beautiful woman who just happened to be bathing on her rooftop at that moment.

Here again we have David in the wrong place. There's nothing wrong with going out to the roof, but as soon as he saw the temptation in Bathsheba, he should have gone back inside! So, in the first two verses, David was already in the wrong place twice. Not only did he look upon Bathsheba as she was bathing, but he pursued her although he knew she was a married woman.

> So David sent and inquired about the woman. And someone said, "Is this not Bathsheba, the daughter of Eliam, the wife of Uriah the Hittite?" Then David sent messengers, and took her; and she came to him, and he lay with her, for she was cleansed from her impurity; and she returned to her house. (2 Samuel 11:3–4)

This is not the end of the story though. Bathsheba became pregnant and what followed was one sin after another as David tried to cover up his adulterous ways, eventually murdering Uriah and incurring God's wrath. (See 2 Samuel 11:5–27; 12:1–4.) All of this happened because David was not in the place God ordained him to be as king—defending his people in battle.

Location...Location...Location

Your position in life means everything to your natural and spiritual well-being. By the word *position*, I mean the point where you happen to be, naturally and spiritually, at any given time. I am not referring to your social standing or career status, even though they can be affected by where you are located.

Some of you reading this book happen to be out of position now because you were out of place in the past. For example, some of you are currently married to the wrong person simply because you were in the wrong neighborhood, the wrong city, or the wrong state at the time when you met. Possibly, you chose your mate because you thought he or she was "the one." Or maybe you felt that person was the best of the group from whom you felt you had to choose. Still others of you are mismatched because you were mesmerized by a dance you had with your mate while out at a party or a club years ago. But really, you had no business being at the club anyway, so you made yourself susceptible to the Enemy's tactics. With your guard down, you married that person, and it has been "hell on earth" ever since!

When living a life for God, position is crucial. Because David was initially out of his proper position, his actions became increasingly complicated, leading him further out of position to one fateful destination—disaster.

Timing Is Everything

Because David was not at war with the rest of the regional kings, because he was out of his designated position, the timing of his life was off. Consequently, every subsequent action he took was not synchronized with God's time and place for him. David was out of step; his rhythm was off. Timing is everything, especially for God's people. It governs and determines the most effective moment for the occurrence of each event in our lives. Remember this:

To everything there is a season, a time for every purpose under heaven....A time to love, and a time to hate; a time of war, and a time of peace. (Ecclesiastes 3:1, 8)

God regulates, monitors, and actually determines the daily direction and the moment-by-moment advances of His people.

Likewise, many Scriptures assure us that God regulates, monitors, and actually determines the daily direction and the moment-by-moment advances of His people:

The steps of a good man are ordered by the LORD, and He delights in his way. (Psalm 37:23)

For the ways of man are before the eyes of the LORD, and He ponders all his paths. (Proverbs 5:21)

In all your ways acknowledge Him, and He shall direct your paths. (Proverbs 3:6)

For David, this was the season to be at war. It was not the time for him to be on his rooftop. Because he was out of his right position and timing, David was vulnerable to the temptation to get out of God's place for him.

Finding Your Proper Place

Where do you belong? Where is your proper location? Where do you fit in? What is your position in life? It is essential that you know.

To discover your position in life, you must first *"set your affection on things above, not on things on the earth"* (Colossians 3:2 KJV). Continually seek God's pleasure and will for your life. In so doing, you will allow His blessings to find you. Wherever the blessings of God overtake you is your proper place to be.

> *Now it shall come to pass, if you diligently obey the voice of the LORD your God, to observe carefully all His commandments which I command you today, that the LORD your God will set you high above all nations of the earth. And all these blessings shall come upon you and overtake you, because you obey the voice of the LORD your God: blessed shall you be in the city, and blessed shall you be in the country.* (Deuteronomy 28:1–3)

At the same time, be conscious of your attitudes, viewpoints, and outlook on life, and be mindful of the choices you make. These all influence your ability to hold and maintain your proper position because they all have consequences, whether good or bad.

Get Out of That Tough Spot

Finally, dear readers, know that a forbidden relationship is never the proper location for you. You must be fully certain that all your relationships—whether in dating, marriage, church fellowship, or casual friendship—meet God's standards and carry His authorization and approval. Guard your choices in this most important matter, and confirm them with the Lord through constant prayer.

However, if you recognize that a relationship of yours is not God-sanctioned, seek the deliverance of God immediately and consistently until you are freed. In the end, you are responsible and will be held accountable for the securing of your life's proper position. It is a place that only you will ever be able to have and to hold perfectly.

Part II

Ties to Avoid:
A Look at Some Not-So-Right Relationships

Introduction to Part II

When looking for lasting love, it is important not only to look at what is good for a relationship but also at what is bad. By examining those relationships that are not desirable or that tear down marriages, we can see what to avoid. Thus, we can define a good relationship *via negativa*, or by what it is not. Defining things by what they are not usually gives a clearer picture of what they are. In this way, I hope to enhance your understanding of what a good romantic relationship is.

At the same time, I hope you will carefully read each of these chapters about negative relationships and examine your own past actions and future tendencies, taking the opportunity to heal from the past and nip any improper thoughts or actions in the bud.

I pray that God will give you wisdom and honesty as you read these pages.

Does Your Yoke Fit?

Chapter Four

Does Your Yoke Fit?

Your search for that special someone or for happiness in your marriage can be made a lot more successful by simply following the guidelines the Bible has already supplied. (It's funny how we forget to do that sometimes.) God has already boomed a resounding "NO" in regard to certain kinds of relationships. There are some relationships that are not pleasing to Him and that He clearly forbids. Among these forbidden relationships are worshiping idols and putting other gods before Him.

You shall have no other gods before Me. You shall not make for yourself a carved image, or any likeness of anything that is in heaven above, or that is in the earth beneath, or that is in the water under the earth; you shall not bow down to them nor serve them. For I, the LORD your God, am a jealous God. (Exodus 20:3–5)

He wants all our worship and all our praise.

Also among the forbidden relationships are things like bestiality, homosexuality, incest, and all sorts of other perversions. We will not be covering these types of relationships here, but they are most definitely forbidden.

One Booming "NO"

Scripture says,

Do not be unequally yoked together with unbelievers. For what fellowship has righteousness with lawlessness? And what communion has light with darkness? And what accord has Christ with Belial? Or what part has a believer with an unbeliever? And what agreement has the temple of God with idols? For you are the temple of the living God. As God has said: "I will dwell in them And walk among them. I will be their God, and they shall be My people." Therefore "Come out from among them and be separate, says the Lord. Do not touch what is unclean, and I will receive you."

(2 Corinthians 6:14–17)

"Do not be yoked with unbelievers." What does that mean exactly? While an ancient Hebrew probably saw a yoke almost every day, today's average man or woman rarely comes into contact with one, and so might not understand the implications of this statement.

According to *Webster's New Collegiate Dictionary*, a yoke is "a wooden bar or frame by which two draft animals (as oxen) are joined at the heads or necks for working together." Before engines and tractors, a farmer would prepare to plow a field by selecting two oxen and yoking them together. After fastening the yoke, he would signal them to plow. If the oxen were not equally strong and did not pull the plow equally, they would create crooked rows, ruining all that hard work.

A marriage requires the joining of two people into one person, but that is impossible to accomplish if you're going in different directions.

The comparison that Paul, the author of Corinthians, is trying to make is that when two people are incompatible in their beliefs, they will end up pulling in opposite directions at different speeds and will be of no use to themselves or anyone else. This applies to many different situations— whom you receive advice from, whom you cooperate with in ministry, whom you form deep friendships with—but most obviously it applies to romantic relationships. After all, a marriage requires the joining of two people into one person, but that is impossible to accomplish if you're going in different directions. For this reason, God has told His children not to marry unbelievers.

A Hard Row to Plow

Though this is one of the most basic commands God has given us concerning marriage—and also one of the most obviously beneficial and wise ones—Christians often think

God went too far when He declared unequally yoked relationships off-limits.

Church pews seem to be increasingly occupied by lonely singles who, as they look within the sphere of the church for their lifetime companions, seem to have the same problem as Adam: *"but for Adam there was not found a helper suitable for him"* (Genesis 2:20 NAS). They end up compromising their Christian standards by expanding the circle of possibilities to include unbelievers. More than likely, the Enemy will have some good-looking, sweet-smelling, silver-tongued devil or vixen ready and willing to lure the believer into a forbidden relationship replete with sensual pleasures and lustful enticements

At this point, duped believers distortedly reason that they had better marry their unbelieving companions rather than fall into sin and, further, that marrying them must be all right with God since the Bible says, *"Because of sexual immorality, let each man have his own wife, and let each woman have her own husband. For it is better to marry than to burn with passion"* (1 Corinthians 7:2, 9).

Yes, Scripture does declare that, but those words in the ninth verse are immediately preceded by this statement: *"But if they cannot exercise self-control, let them marry."* First and foremost, we are to strive for self-control.

Moreover, the whole context of the passage shows that Paul was writing to Christians who may not have been gifted by God with celibacy yet wanted to live pure, godly lives. He still cautioned them, however, not to go seeking mates, with the implication that they were to wait for the Lord to provide for their needs and to bring about any change in their marital status. He also clearly stated that they were free to marry whom they wished, but *"only in the Lord"* (v. 39). Thus, Christians need to exercise self-control at the outset of any encounter with an unbeliever. It is much easier not to take the first steps that might somehow lead to unequal yoking than it is to break the bonds that have formed once an intimate relationship has developed.

That still doesn't satisfy the heart that views God as harsh and judgmental in His prohibitions. Yet, as our loving heavenly Father, God wants only what is best for His children, and He knows that some situations lead to terrible heartache and ultimate disaster. Only because He wants to protect us from having to suffer the dire consequences of wrong relationships does He forbid certain alliances. By His merciful warning, God gives us the knowledge to avoid the Enemy's waiting trap, which is baited with the poison of the forbidden.

> As our loving heavenly Father, God wants only what is best for His children, and He knows that some situations lead to terrible heartache and ultimate disaster.

Let's take a look at a biblical example of why God commands what he does about being unequally yoked.

Strange Women

When you stop and think, it seems rather unusual that Samson would love *"strange women"* (1 Kings 11:1 KJV). After all, he was a Nazirite, an Israelite who took a vow of separation and self-imposed abstinence in order to consecrate himself for a special purpose. (For Samson, that special purpose always involved some specific task in the service of God that would benefit His people.) Given Samson's sacred pledge and the fact that even Israelites who were not Nazirites were commanded not to marry the people of Canaan (see Exodus 34:11, 16; Deuteronomy 7:1, 3), why was it that the three great female loves of his life—his Timnite wife, a Gazite harlot, and the infamous Delilah—were all Philistines, the Israelites' most notorious enemies and definitely on the taboo list? Precisely because they were forbidden!

Despite the special calling on his life, Samson, like many of us, seemed to gravitate toward what was no good for him. The things he could not have became more desirable because they were off-limits. Clearly, Samson's renowned physical strength had its counterpoint in moral weakness. Willfully, in full knowledge of his sacred covenant with God, Samson entered forbidden relationship after forbidden relationship with the pagan Philistine women. His vow and covenant, however, specified that Samson live a sanctified lifestyle, in which he would not cut his hair, drink strong drink, or touch anything considered unclean, including strange women:

When either a man or woman consecrates an offering to take the vow of a Nazirite, to separate himself to the LORD, he shall separate himself from wine and similar drink; he shall drink neither vinegar made from wine nor vinegar made from similar drink; neither shall he drink any grape juice, nor eat fresh grapes or raisins. All the days of his separation he shall eat nothing that is produced by the grapevine, from seed to skin. All the days of the vow of his separation no razor shall come upon his head; until the days are fulfilled for which he separated himself to the LORD, he shall be holy. Then he shall let the locks of the hair of his head grow. All the days that he separates himself to the LORD he shall not go near a dead body. He shall not make himself unclean even for his father or his mother, for his brother or his sister, when they die, because his separation to God is on his head. All the days of his separation he shall be holy to the LORD. This is the law of the Nazirite who vows to the LORD the offering for his separation, and besides that, whatever else his hand is able to provide; according to the vow which he takes, so he must do according to the law of his separation.

(Numbers 6:2–8, 21)

[Like] *king Solomon* [Samson] *loved many strange women...of the nations concerning which the LORD said unto the children of Israel, Ye shall not go in to them, neither shall they come in unto you: for surely they will turn away your heart after their gods.*

(1 Kings 11:1–2 KJV)

Ultimately, by pursuing the unholy thing that he could not have, the world's strongest man lost the vehicle through which his holy empowerment was manifested—his hair!

Samson's hair was the symbol of his Nazarite pledge. When a person decided to become a Nazarite, whether for a short period of time or for his entire life, he was required to stop cutting and shaving his hair. When the period of the pledge was over, the Nazarite's hair was shaved off and burned at the temple because his unshaved hair was the sign of his vow, and now his vow was over.

Samson, however, had taken his Nazarite vow for life. His hair should never have been shaven. Additionally, the superhuman strength God had given him in order to deliver the Israelites from the Philistines was connected to his hair. If his hair was shaved, that was it—he would lose his strength. Unfortunately, Delilah, the object of Samson's last forbidden love, worked to make sure this would happen. (See Judges 16:4–20.)

Duped by a Damsel

The most commonly known relationship that Samson had with a Philistine woman is the one he shared with Delilah. This foreign woman became the channel through which the terrified Philistines ultimately sapped the very thing that caused them to tremble and made Samson exceptional—his superhuman strength.

Despite the special calling on his life, Samson, like many of us, seemed to gravitate toward what was no good for him. The things he could not have became more desirable because they were off-limits.

Delilah, who was hardly as true to Samson as he was to her, could be bought! Each of the Philistine lords offered her some three thousand dollars to discover and reveal to them the sacred secret of Samson's strength. Falling victim to her seductive control and his own lusts, Samson could not perceive the methodical efficiency by which this calculating woman went about earning her weight in silver through betrayal.

By using the feminine version of the manipulative ploy, "If you love and want me, you'll do what I ask," Delilah was able to insist that Samson tell her what she desired to hear. She persuaded him to cross the point of no return, which was the breaking of his godly vow and covenant. The pestering, vexing Delilah eventually pressed Samson into revealing to her that the secret to his strength lay in his glorious, uncut hair. Upon acquiring this knowledge, Delilah turned on Samson and had his head shaved, which allowed him to be taken into captivity by the waiting Philistines.

All of a sudden, Samson was bound and could no longer fight off his enemies. Taking a quick mental check, Samson must have surely wondered why God had taken his strength from him. And as quickly as he wondered, he knew: Because he had reneged on his vow to God. The covenant had been broken, and his strength had been removed.

In sharing first his flesh and then his secret with the Philistine woman, Samson severed his binding covenant with God and lost his strength. The revelatory fact, however, is that long before Samson uttered the sacred truth of his vow to Delilah, his real strength—his spiritual strength—had already begun to dwindle. His moral might had actually started to dissipate when he first began to sidestep the conditions of his vow. Samson's tampering with the covenant began with his initial attraction to Philistine women.

Now Samson went down to Timnah, and saw a woman in Timnah of the daughters of the Philistines. So he went up and told his father and mother, saying, "I have

seen a woman in Timnah of the daughters of the Phi-
listines; now therefore, get her for me as a wife." Then
his father and mother said to him, "Is there no woman
among the daughters of your brethren, or among all my
people, that you must go and get a wife from the uncir-
cumcised Philistines?" And Samson said to his father,
"Get her for me, for she pleases me well."

(Judges 14:1–3)

Marrying a Philistine did not satisfy Samson's desire for the forbidden. His intensifying interest in these prohibited women culminated in his attraction to Delilah, yet his escalating lust slowly but surely weakened his invisible strength of will, character, morality, virtue, discernment, and judgment.

The High Cost of Entertaining the Forbidden

Eve was doomed when she first entertained the Devil's conversation, long before the actual partaking of forbidden fruit. Likewise, Samson's moral strength began to abate long before he actually revealed his secret to Delilah and subsequently lost his physical strength. For Samson, the real loss came when he broke his vow. The source of Samson's strength was not so much in his hair as it was in the power of the covenant that existed between him and God.

We are all walking in a unique covenant with God if we have accepted Jesus as our Lord and Savior.

We are all walking in a unique covenant with God if we have accepted Jesus as our Lord and Savior. He is our true Bridegroom, and to accept an earthly spouse who is not in His plan for us is to violate our agreement. We must be sure to walk honorably in our covenants. Realize that there is no relationship good enough to cause you to violate that covenant with God or to lose the strength that is found in keeping your vows to Him.

> *That which has gone from your lips you shall keep and perform, for you voluntarily vowed to the LORD your God what you have promised with your mouth.*
> (Deuteronomy 23:23)
>
> *Therefore keep the words of this covenant, and do them, that you may prosper in all that you do.*
> (Deuteronomy 29:9)

Samson paid a mighty price for his forbidden relationship with Delilah. There were consequences. It will be the same for you if you pursue a relationship with an unbeliever. For many, the price will be paid in a broken heart, a shattered marriage, or a lifetime of loneliness in which you are unable to share the closeness with your spouse that results when both of you worship the same Lord. For some, the cost has been less formidable. Yet, all have had to pay the exorbitant price of losing fellowship with God. No matter how you entertain them, forbidden relationships cost too much!

The Marriage Side of the Coin

Now all this talk about being unequally yoked is not to say that if you are already married to an unbeliever you should divorce him or her immediately. Quite the contrary: Your marriage is a contract, a solid agreement, and you should honor that. Maybe your decision to enter into marriage with an unbeliever was a faulty one, or maybe you became a Christian after marriage but your spouse has yet to find the Lord. Either way, you made an agreement and you must follow through. Paul taught this in his first letter to the Corinthians.

If any brother has a wife who does not believe, and she is willing to live with him, let him not divorce her. And a woman who has a husband who does not believe, if he is willing to live with her, let her not divorce him. For the unbelieving husband is sanctified by the wife, and the unbelieving wife is sanctified by the husband; otherwise your children would be unclean, but now they are holy. But if the unbeliever departs, let him depart; a brother or a sister is not under bondage in such cases. But God has called us to peace. For how do you know, O wife, whether you will save your husband? Or how do you know, O husband, whether you will save your wife? (1 Corinthians 7:12–16)

I do not doubt that God will make you a blessing to your mate if you allow Him to, providing your mate with an ample witness of the love and salvation available through Him.

5

Castles in the Sky: A Woman's Tendencies

Chapter Five

Castles in the Sky: A Woman's Tendencies

Relationships that are not based in reality can be as unhealthy and dangerous as those that are forbidden. Especially for females, imagined love and self-created romance can lead to emotional ruin. On the other hand, men are often susceptible to manufacturing flawless female fantasy figures and then becoming overly attached to the distorted objects of their own making. Many people waste great depth of feeling on a love that doesn't truly exist—except in their minds. The unfortunate fantasizer can be robbed of the opportunity to ever experience genuine love and affection, due to dashed expectations or an unobtainable, impossible dream. This can happen both inside and outside of marriage.

When imagination runs amok and a fantasy goes too far, it can become an actual reality for the disillusioned creator of the image. The fantasizer then begins to modify the real world in order to fit the illusion. Mentally, events are changed, conversations are revised, mistakes are corrected, blunders are perfected, flaws are airbrushed, gestures are distorted, and intentions are altered to adapt to the imaginary scenario. Eventually, this perfect fantasy relationship becomes so much better than any conflicting, imperfect, natural union could ever be that the person begins to dwell in the realm of the imagination rather than flesh-and-blood reality.

> When imagination runs amok and a fantasy goes too far, it can become an actual reality for the disillusioned creator of the image.

A fleeting thought can lead to idle daydreaming, which in turn can develop into distorted imaginations and finally to the formation of delusional strongholds. Such is the progression with fantasy relationships. Based on the deception of the Enemy instead of God's truth, these illusory associations can form powerful connections in the mind of the creator even though they are not real. According to Scripture, these thoughts must be broken up and cast down. Thankfully, God has not only shown us how to do it, but He has also given us helpful preventative measures to implement as well:

> *For though we walk in the flesh, we do not war according to the flesh. For the weapons of our warfare are not carnal but mighty in God for pulling down strongholds, casting down arguments ["imaginations" KJV] and every high thing that exalts itself against the knowledge of God, bringing every thought into captivity to the obedience of Christ.* (2 Corinthians 10:3–5)

When we learn to bring that first fleeting romantic thought *"into captivity to the obedience of Christ"* by praying and seeking the Lord's wisdom about it, we will develop discernment about what we are thinking. Not every thought that we have about the opposite sex or a particular member of it will head us in the wrong direction. However, the earlier we can check out our thoughts with the Lord, the easier it will be to dismiss them when they are not godly. In this way, we can break the destructive cycle at the introduction of the "harmless" thought before our imaginations take over and strongholds are formed. The process is the same when tearing down strongholds that have become entrenched, although it is more difficult to accomplish because of their strength.

Learning how Christians can get caught in the cages of fantasy relationships is one of the best ways to avoid the same traps. And knowing there is a way out if you have become ensnared will give you strength to tear down your strongholds of illusion and delusion. May God grant you the grace and wisdom never to settle for a shadow of a relationship when He will give you the real thing.

Living the Daydream

Often in instances of fantasized love, women's own emotionalism, vulnerability to conversation, and tendencies to be receptive to what comes from men—attention, affection, encouragement—make them susceptible to developing imaginary relationships. Although plenty of men in the world deliberately and knowingly lead women on, impressionable women frequently mistake gentlemen's courteous treatment of ladies for signals of personal interest. In need of male attention, women who are lonely tend to latch on to any civility or act of good manners, taking such behavior personally and then mentally blowing it out of proportion. A woman's natural receptive tendency to internalize what she hears from a man and how she is approached by a man can lead to her daydreaming about him and embellishing on the events.

Spurred on by romance novels and popular love songs, with their tales of love at first sight and damsels being rescued by gallant knights, a woman's longing for adoration can grow to such an extent that her mind starts to fabricate a romantic relationship, which supplies the dynamics that are missing in her life.

> *For of this sort are those who creep into households and make captives of gullible women loaded down with sins, led away by various lusts.* (2 Timothy 3:6)

A married woman may then begin to think that the reality she lives with her husband is just not the dream she was destined to live. She may begin to the think she didn't find "the one." This can devastate a marriage.

A single woman may take the ideal romances she sees in the movies so seriously that she develops an unrealistic notion of how a relationship works and what Mr. Right should look and act like. The faultless actor becomes her ideal, and she rejects any suitors who don't match up—which is all of them!

A woman's natural receptive tendency to internalize what she hears from a man can lead to her daydreaming about him and embellishing on the events.

Or perhaps the single woman's fantasy rests on a real flesh-and-blood man, one who seems to embody everything that is good and perfect, and she misinterprets his friendliness as something more, passing up what could have been healthy relationships for a misguided dream. This is what happened to April, the woman who describes in the following story how she created for herself a distorted reality of love.

Someday My Prince Will Come

My name is April. For some time I was involved in a great relationship, the type most people yearn to have once in their lifetime. Tom and I met very casually one Monday morning as we both tried to squeeze into the same crowded elevator of the office building where I worked. My career as a junior account executive (a glorified label for a marketing assistant) for the largest advertising agency in town was going nowhere fast—that is, until that fateful day when Tom came to work at the same firm.

Since we had already met, the boss asked me to introduce Tom to everyone and acquaint him with the general office procedures. In those couple of hours, Tom and I got to know each other much better than coworkers generally do in a year or two. His personality was so open and his demeanor was so genuinely caring that I told him about my frustrations with my job and the "good old boy" network. With overbearing, cavalier arrogance, the account executives—and especially my immediate boss—would repeatedly dismiss my ideas as being unimaginative or trite behind closed doors, but then they would plagiarize them with clients, claiming personal credit for my original concepts.

Tom was assigned to my design team, but it was obvious from the start that he was being groomed to take over the position of our accounts manager, who was in turn going to be bumped up the corporate ladder. Nevertheless, Tom was always forthright with our boss, attributing winning ideas to the originator even when he could have easily maintained they were his. At the time I failed to notice that he was impartial with his encouragement and acknowledgment of the efforts of everyone on the design team. All I could see was that Tom not only liked my work but had also graciously risen to my defense with the boss on more than one occasion. I felt protected and valued for the first time in years.

Within a few months, Tom was officially promoted to the position of account executive, thus becoming the director of our design team and my new boss. With this change in status and power, Tom's demeanor remained the same. He was always friendly, encouraging, and caring. He took into consideration our individual needs and circumstances, never demanding that we give up our personal lives for the sake of a project but always eliciting from each of us the maximum of our potential.

In the atmosphere of Tom's support and reassurance, my once wounded ego began to heal and my sagging mood lifted. As I felt better about myself and my self-esteem grew, my creativity blossomed. My input on projects became more valuable, and clients started choosing my sales campaign ideas with regularity. I was flourishing personally and professionally, thanks to Tom.

A woman's fantasy may rest on a man who seems to embody everything that is good and perfect, and she misinterprets his friendliness as something more.

Tom began to take me along to client meetings and business luncheons. A new side of me emerged in those situations. Normally rather shy in social settings, I began to be at ease with clients, conversing warmly and developing a rapport with them. In what is ordinarily a scary, cutthroat world in which everyone is out to undermine everyone else, Tom valued my growth and provided opportunities for my advancement.

However, what was more important to me was the exhilarating feeling I got every time Tom complimented my appearance or held the door open for me. Previously, I had thought that such courtesies were demeaning to women, but now his impeccable manners made me feel desirable as a woman.

Sporadically, Tom invited me to lunch to discuss a particular project we were working on. He also called me at home on rare occasions after work for the same reason. Of course, the personal side of our lives crept into the conversations we shared. We enjoyed each other's company and grew to be great friends. He became my wise counselor as well as my mentor.

As our relationship was becoming increasingly friendly, my feelings toward him were intensifying. At home in my apartment, I mulled over Tom's every comment, every kind gesture, every knowing look, and I smiled with each thought. Each morning and evening, I thanked God for bringing Tom into my life and asked for His blessing on our friendship.

About now, some of you might be thinking to yourselves, "Oh, isn't that sweet? What a beautiful love story!" But, I am sorry to say, the story does not end here. In fact, it is only the beginning of a new chapter in my life, a chapter I had no intention of writing.

Because Tom had once left a message on my answering machine when I was out shopping, I began to stay at home in case he needed to reach me. I made up excuses not to go to dinner or the movies with my friends. I even stopped going to my church's midweek Bible studies, which I loved. I told myself that the current client's business was vital to our agency, that we were in a crucial stage of design development, and that it was essential for me to be available as much as possible—for the good of the company and my career, of course.

Living in Dreamland

Home alone, I dreamed of what it would be like when Tom would finally reveal his attraction to me. The chemistry between us was so strong that I was convinced he experienced it, too. Because of his special care and kindness to me, I was sure the interest was mutual.

Intimate conversations played over and over in my mind. His voice alone excited me. More than once, even though no one else could hear, I burst out laughing as I remembered one of his jokes! We talked about everything intensely. Our bond grew closer as we spoke from our hearts, sharing our secret dreams and desires. As we gave ourselves emotionally and mentally, I knew that this compassionate, gentle man had won a place in my heart. Increasingly, I found my world revolving around him.

As I listened to him, I envisioned that I was a pillow for Tom—someone to soothe him, someone to provide peace, someone for him just to lean and rest on. I liked taking on that role because I wanted to be his special confidante, the person he turned to as his only trusted intimate.

There were many reasons why I was falling in love with him. He was a man who was strong, powerful, and authoritative, but at the same time he was caring, gentle, and expressive. When others admired his charisma, I was able to stand back and smile because I knew him. He was my friend.

Many times I wondered what he saw in me. We were two different people with two totally different personalities. He was open; I was closed. He was boisterous; I was quiet. He was outgoing; I was reserved. A girlfriend of mine who knew him once told me that because of the type of man he was, he probably had hundreds on his list of friends and that she was sure I was at the bottom of the list. She added that if all of his friends were ever in a room together, I would probably be the least visible.

Still, our relationship had grown to the point where I felt it was safe to believe I was the sole object of his affection, his girl. However, I tended to forget that someone had already beaten me to the first-place position in his life—his wife. Yes, Tom was a married man.

I had met Tom's wife a few times at agency parties, but hidden hostility lurked behind my curious smile when we were introduced. She became my rival. I resented the fact that she was legally attached to him. I needed him, too! He made me feel good about myself; he made me laugh; he cared about me, and I about him. I hated the fact that whenever she was present, Tom quickly shoved me backstage, yet when the curtain reopened, I was expected to do my song-and-dance routine as usual. Eventually, I could not play the understudy anymore. I was hurting and was tired of being the supporting actress. I wanted the leading role!

Getting the Shock of My Life

This predicament led to the only argument that Tom and I ever had. He had arranged a dinner party at a posh restaurant to entertain a potential client and help secure the account for our firm. Tom wanted the entire creative team to be there, with spouses or suitable dates. Since I had previously withdrawn from the dating scene, Tom suggested that I be escorted by a recently divorced member of the client's staff. Of course, I knew that Tom's wife would accompany him, and I was not sure that I could handle seeing them together.

Despite my inner conflict, I accepted the invitation. I was nervous, my palms were slightly damp, and my smile was completely phony. I did not want to say or do the wrong thing in her presence. Throughout the evening, I wondered what she was thinking about me. Did she see that I was too closely attached to her husband? Could she tell that I loved Tom? I tried to act nonchalant and show an interest in my escort, but I knew I was doing a poor job of covering up my real feelings.

As I covertly studied the way Tom was so solicitous of his wife, my great friendship with him seemed to collapse right in front of my eyes. Everything I had worked so hard to build was crumbling, and I had become unimportant. The curtain had been drawn on me, the leading actress was onstage, and I had to fade into the background and wait my turn again. But I had reached the end of my rope! I refused to play second fiddle anymore.

At that moment, I hated him for putting me in a position where I had to compete for his attention and love. Why couldn't we talk like we used to? Why had I suddenly become invisible? Was I simply a thing of convenience for him? I was so angry that I was about ready to explode. If it meant losing my special friend, I would be devastated, but so be it!

The night finally ended with Tom and I creating a scene—we got in a quarrel over the waiter's tip! Can you believe that? It was unbelievably silly. And it had absolutely nothing to do with the waiter; it was all about us. I don't remember all the details of what happened, but I know that I insisted and he insisted; I argued and he argued back, both mad as hornets! The debate ended with me storming out of the restaurant, leaving a perplexed Tom to smooth things over with the client.

The following day was Sunday, and I followed my regular Sunday routine, but my heart was heavy. I barely heard a word of the sermon because, throughout the day, I kept questioning myself, "How could I have been so stupid? What had I expected to happen, anyway? I knew all along he was married!"

I went through my daily routines in silence. No one noticed my pain. I felt so used, so betrayed, so overwhelmed. My only release was in the form of warm, silent tears.

I took a personal leave from work so I would not have to face Tom. A week or so later, he called to see if I was all right, but he really wanted to talk about what had happened that night. When I finally admitted how I felt about him and that I was threatened by his wife's presence, he apologized for ever having done anything to give me the impression that he was attracted to me in a romantic way. He let me know that he was totally in love with his wife, his commitment to her was sacred, and he would never violate her trust in him.

At that moment, I felt as if Tom had suddenly slapped me. However, the shock of his words forced me out of my delusion and brought me back to reality. My mind slowly grasped the truth that our romance existed only in my imagination.

Returning to Earth

As a result of this fantasy, I have been on an emotional roller coaster, I have faced many days with uneasiness, and

I have endured endless self-interrogation in a quest for personal authenticity. How could I have spent countless hours talking with him and being treated like a queen, a priceless jewel, a precious gem, and not indulged in that relationship all the more? It was impossible!

Yet, I had to admit I had deceived myself. Tom had never misrepresented his intentions toward me or singled me out for any special treatment. He had always been a gentleman and had never given me any indication that he was interested in me in an intimate sense. Out of loneliness, perhaps, I had misread his actions and had just let my imagination run wild.

I had to deal with the reality of the situation. This man was simply not mine to love. He belonged to someone else, and I had to accept that fact. Deep down, I knew that God would never have blessed our relationship because He never endorses sin.

I have come to the place of repentance for desiring something outside of God's will and for not trusting God to supply all my needs, including romance and genuine love. I am learning daily to focus on the truth of God's Word and to capture every thought and bring it to Christ before my imagination gets me into another awkward, painful situation.

Flesh, Lies, and the Devil

We could engage in a heated debate over the origins of fantasies such as these that have become strongholds. Some people emphatically declare that Satan is the original source, since *"he is a liar and the father of it"* (John 8:44), and since it is no secret that he desires *"to deceive, if possible, even the elect"* (Matthew 24:24). Others insist just as strongly that our own carnal nature gets us in this trouble. They cite that in our *"flesh nothing good dwells"* (Romans 7:18), that man's *"heart is deceitful above all things, and desperately wicked"* (Jeremiah 17:9), and that as a man *"thinks in his heart, so is he"* (Proverbs 23:7).

Strongholds are erected in our minds by the combined efforts of Satan and our own carnality.

I believe that strongholds are erected in our minds by the combined efforts of Satan and our own carnality. The Devil tempts us where we are most vulnerable, and our *"flesh with its passions and desires"* (Galatians 5:24) latches on, if only in the recesses of the mind. As this process is repeated, a mental structure eventually takes shape and is reinforced, becoming a haven in which to hide our pet delusions and distorted thought patterns.

However, if we are truly born again, we are no longer just passive spectators in these circumstances, simply reacting to Satan's lures. We have a choice in the matter as to who is going to control our lives and how we are going to live.

> *For those who live according to the flesh set their minds on the things of the flesh, but those who live according to the Spirit, the things of the Spirit. For to be carnally minded is death, but to be spiritually minded is life and peace. Because the carnal mind is enmity against God; for it is not subject to the law of God, nor indeed can be.* (Romans 8:5–7)

Remember that it is quite possible to be a Christian and still be carnally minded, *"indulging the desires of the flesh and of the mind"* (Ephesians 2:3 NAS). Paul wrote to the early church at Corinth, *"I, brethren, could not speak to you as to spiritual people but as to carnal, as to babes in Christ...for you are still carnal"* (1 Corinthians 3:1, 3). However, those words are in the middle of a passage on gaining spiritual discernment, wisdom, and instructions for laying the proper foundations for living. In other words, Christians are to grow up spiritually and become mature enough to make choices through the all-wise guidance of the Holy Spirit and not through their ignorant flesh.

> *But put on the Lord Jesus Christ, and make no provision for the flesh, to fulfill its lusts.* (Romans 13:14)

> *Set your mind on things above, not on things on the earth. For you died, and your life is hidden with Christ in God.* (Colossians 3:2–3)

Our loving heavenly Father has not left us to refocus our minds on our own. Since our lives are hidden in Him, we can choose to respond to His voice and to walk in His vision for our lives. The Lord wants us to be involved in the most fulfilling, intimate, exciting relationships possible—first with Him and then with the person of His choosing.

6

Castles in the Sky: A Man's Tendencies

Chapter Six

Castles in the Sky: A Man's Tendencies

en are not immune to forming unrealistic relationship ideas. They also can suffer from fantasy perception of others, and often of themselves. Men can be just as immature, impractical, or psychologically imbalanced as women sometimes are—and just as susceptible to "living the lie" that their imagination tells them. And the fact is that even men who strive to follow Christ are not always exempt from this tragedy.

In deciphering the different mental, psychological, and sensual tendencies of the sexes, I have observed that where women are primarily moved by what they hear, men are mostly affected by what they see. The visual information a man receives is what motivates, inspires, stimulates, and arouses him, especially when it relates to the opposite sex.

The eyes of man are never satisfied. (Proverbs 27:20)

But I say to you that whoever looks at a woman to lust for her has already committed adultery with her in his heart. (Matthew 5:28)

With the certain understanding that men are primarily visual creatures, then, it is easy to pinpoint the origins and substance of their flights of fancy about females. Quite often, men's fantasies are based on those superficial standards that are established by sight.

Imaginary Goddess

While "Ms. Right" for the average man is usually a composite of select traits in a number of areas—including spirituality, personality, disposition, background, interests, and physical appearance—the fantasy creator only cares about one trait in a woman: her appearance. She is an unrealistic creature of his imagination, a self-designed goddess whose existence and availability is never likely to extend beyond the confines of the creator's mind. This ideal female may be based upon a teacher or an older woman who impressed the man in his youth; a celebrity or fashion model who has been awarded sex-symbol status by the media; some other isolated, far-removed woman who is generally unobtainable by the man, such as an attractive lady he has met in the work arena; or a two-dimensional image, airbrushed to perfection, presented to him through the perverted realms of pornography.

Secular psychologists and therapists generally encourage the regular practice of daydreaming and fantasizing, telling us that having a "healthy imagination" is, in fact, healthy. Where the Christian man is concerned, however, an overdeveloped habit or tendency to create mental realities is nothing less than futile imagination. The Word of God clearly speaks against this practice because it is often a hindrance to the believer's spiritual growth and can open the door to perversion.

Quite often, men's fantasies are based on those superficial standards that are established by sight.

Although they knew God, they did not glorify Him as God, nor were thankful, but became futile in their thoughts ["vain in their imaginations" KJV], and their foolish hearts were darkened....Therefore God also gave them up to uncleanness, in the lusts of their hearts, to dishonor their bodies among themselves....For this reason God gave them up to vile passions. For even their women exchanged the natural use for what is against nature. Likewise also the men, leaving the natural use of the woman, burned in their lust...committing what is shameful, and receiving in themselves the penalty of their error which was due. (Romans 1:21, 24, 26–27)

Keeping Up Appearances

A popular truism within the circles of human psychology is that when a man follows after the unrealistic feminine images of his mind and exclusively seeks women of physical perfection for companionship, it frequently is a sign that he feels severely inadequate in some aspect of his manhood. A preoccupation with the superficial—those temporal elements of outward appearance that are subject to change with time and have little to do with the establishment of long-term, successful relationships—also suggests a fear of intimacy, sexual and personal insecurity, and a certain lack of self-esteem.

Another explanation is that the man who follows his fantasies may be an extremely high-minded, arrogant individual. In either case, these men distortedly believe that they are all the more manly when they have acquired or are accompanied by a certain type of female. The man who must have a "trophy woman" draped on his arm needs her in order to feel he can successfully compete with his male peers. He may use his female companion to provoke other men's jealousy of him for his capturing such a great-looking "prize."

Such is a most unhealthy and ungodly mentality, a perverse way of viewing women. This behavior, which is the result of a stronghold having been allowed to develop, must be cast down—and cast out—especially from the church, since it does not suit the man who professes salvation.

For the weapons of our warfare are not carnal but mighty in God for pulling down strongholds, casting down arguments ["imaginations" KJV] and every high thing that exalts itself against the knowledge of God, bringing every thought into captivity to the obedience of Christ, and being ready to punish all disobedience when your obedience is fulfilled. Do you look at things according to the outward appearance? If anyone is convinced in himself that he is Christ's, let him again consider this in himself, that just as he is Christ's, even so we are Christ's. (2 Corinthians 10:4–7)

Some men distortedly believe that they are all the more manly when they have acquired or are accompanied by a certain type of female.

The man who thus objectifies women unquestionably has a womanizing attitude. Often, he is not above mentally or physically abusing the females he becomes involved with, since his motives for securing them in relationships are selfish and shallow and he himself is insecure. Moreover, if he is not a user and abuser of women, the man who takes his fantasies for reality is usually a romantic failure of some sort, one whose self-perception is boosted only when a beautiful woman is on his arm.

Impossible Standards

No one is good enough for these men of unrealistic and unnatural standards. Requiring that a woman be of a certain complexion, weight, height, hair style, and eye color, or that she succumb to other idiosyncrasies and personal fetishes, many men in the world and in the church are rating women on biased scales of one to ten. They are seeking their mates, not for how virtuous, God-fearing, and sound of character they are, but for how these women can make them look good and satisfy them sexually.

The sad irony, however, is that such men are rarely the physical counterparts of the female types they idolize and set as ideals! Wanting her to be beautiful, he is often none too handsome. She must be fit and trim, but he can have an overinflated "spare tire" hanging over his belt. While she must be dressed to reveal her best features and have her makeup and hair done to perfection, he is often anything but the epitome of good grooming.

Overall, these men ask and desire of women what they themselves cannot offer. If their excessive demands are not met, they become content with the distorted fantasy images in their minds, resigning themselves to permanent, though unfulfilling, relationships with figments of their imaginations. Feeling that they cannot find an available woman to meet their qualifications or that no suitable woman exists who fits their ideal image, they settle for being in love with themselves.

> *Likewise also the men, leaving the natural use of the woman, burned in their lust for one another, men with men committing what is shameful, and receiving in themselves the penalty of their error which was due. And even as they did not like to retain God in their knowledge, God gave them over to a debased ["reprobate" KJV] mind, to do those things which are not fitting.* (Romans 1:27–28)

Cruising the Pews

It is with a bit of reluctance that I tell the following story. I was indirectly involved in this scenario, but it has as its central character a fellow whom I will call Rich and who happens to be a close friend of mine. This incident happened in the church where I serve as pastor, and I only share it now because of its timely illustration of how the fantasy phenomenon plays out with men, and particularly with men in the church. This man did not outwardly appear to have a problem with unrealistic fantasies, but an unexpected turn of events brought to light this individual's distorted mindset and womanizing tendencies.

Be sure your sin will find you out. (Numbers 32:23)

For there is nothing hidden which will not be revealed, nor has anything been kept secret but that it should come to light. (Mark 4:22)

Rich, the "young" man in question, was about forty-three years old when his immaturity was inadvertently displayed through his adolescent dealings with females in our church. A divorced father of four, Rich is a person I have known well for many years. In the opinions of many people, he is a hardworking, all-around good person.

Nevertheless, the not-so-good side of my friend and parishioner began to dawn on me during a Thanksgiving dinner event sponsored by our church one year. This was an occasion where families both inside and outside the church were to be blessed with good food and fellowship, an event that most attendees clearly understood to be a "dress-up" affair. Much to my embarrassment, however, Rich for some reason decided that his attire would be casual. He came to the dinner dressed in jeans, sneakers, an open shirt, and a flashy gold necklace.

Needless to say, Rich's behavior angered me considerably. Not only had he openly ignored and disregarded the established dress code, but since he was a rather visible figure in the church, he was a role model for many. In addition, he was a prominent participant in the festivities taking place that very evening!

Feeling that they cannot find an available woman to meet their qualifications or that no suitable woman exists who fits their ideal image, some men settle for being in love with themselves.

I confronted Rich frankly and expressed to him my serious displeasure and disappointment in his casual attire and attitude. I relayed to him the general consensus of all who saw him there that night: that he looked like a young, careless teenager. "Grow up!" I angrily admonished him, before walking away. Little did I realize, however, that this brother's inappropriate dress was an external indication of a deeper, more serious, internal problem, involving a lack of accountability and responsibility on his part. And I certainly had no clue that this small incident with him was just a preview of an even greater discrepancy that would surface and erupt later on.

A few months later that bigger situation reared its ugly head. To my great disappointment, several young women in the church made a general complaint to me that Rich was in the habit of making romantic overtures to each of them. According to these young ladies, who were all either in their late teens or early twenties, if Rich was not complimenting them excessively on their appearance, he was asking them overly intimate questions, extending personal invitations to private dinners, or trying to arrange meetings in other remote settings. Many times, his conversations with these young women contained inappropriate, suggestive overtones. He had even offered his personal telephone number to more than one girl and had paid visits to at least two of them at their workplaces.

The overall problem that these women had with Rich was twofold. First of all, while he was old enough to be their father, or at least a protective authority figure in their lives, he was choosing to flirt with them. Second, if he were indeed the type of man who preferred a younger woman, this might have been acceptable except for the fact that he obviously preferred younger women, plural. He refused to single out and to pursue an interest in just one of them. Instead, he was attempting to seduce all of them at the same time!

Since I am the pastor of a growing and varied congregation, I try to be sensitive to and understanding of the needs of all of my parishioners, married and single. While I do emphasize to my congregation that the church is not a social club or a singles bar, it is my sincere desire to see all of my members happy, healthy, and honorably situated in the area of romance. It has never been my habit to dictate to individuals whom they could or could not entertain, date, and court as potential partners. Simply put, such is not my place or jurisdiction.

At the same time, however, God has given me the responsibility of providing a spiritual covering for the entire congregation. This often involves protecting those who do not have a covering in the natural, as with these young ladies. Thus, I occasionally have to challenge men who try to infiltrate and contaminate the church with the woman-izing tactics and tendencies they employ out in the world to seduce unwitting, unfortunate females. I make no apologies for adamantly refusing to allow such behavior and practices to have free course and rein in the house of the Lord! In this case, I was absolutely compelled to confront Rich with the allegations of these young women, all of whom, again, were between the very tender ages of seventeen and twenty-four!

Prior to this incident, I had been alerted to his less-than-honorable feelings toward women, and specifically toward those single women in our church. On occasion, we had openly and honestly talked about his single status and his desire for a permanent companion. It was an issue of serious concern for my friend and brother in the Lord. He wanted and needed a wife. I had given him certain prophetic assurances that the woman God had secured for him would eventually make her appearance, and that when she did, this brother would know her immediately by the intense feelings of pro-tectiveness he would have toward her. Desiring to make his own permanent mark in the life of this particular woman, he would not want any other men talking to her!

The church is not a social club or a singles bar.

This utterance on my part was not made with the intent of encouraging Rich to be possessive or jealous concerning the future woman. Rather, it was given to help him know that once she had entered his life, this woman was God's choice for him; to enable him to identify that she was indeed the one by the magnitude of his feelings; and to offer him comfort in the knowledge that waiting on the Lord would truly pay off in due time.

God's Gift to Women?

Waiting, of course, was the operative word here. It was not very long before this brother gave in to impatience, doubt, and arrogance concerning single women in our church and his future possibilities with any of them. After one particularly stirring Sunday service, Rich informed me that he would never find a good woman among those in our membership because all of the ladies there were, in his opinion, "too bossy, too independent, too demanding, or too stuck on themselves."

Again angered by his ungracious, disrespectful attitude, I asked him, "Do you think that you are God's gift to women? Do you really believe you have so much to offer a female in terms of stability, good looks, and romance that none of the single women in the church is deserving, worthy, or good enough for you?" I demanded a truthful answer from him!

Immediately detecting the sarcasm in my dogmatic questioning, Rich backed down from his haughty outlook and made a desperate attempt to retrieve his negative statement through an apology. At his admission of his own imperfection, I let him alone, but from then on, I was fully alerted to and ever mindful of his unacceptable views about the opposite sex.

My second cause for concern was, quite honestly, that Rich was too mature in years to have exclusive interest in girls from such a youthful age bracket. The fact of the matter was that he had been a grown man before the oldest of these young ladies was even born!

While it is true that age is only a number between many couples, it is a rare man who can properly see to the needs of a female twenty years—or more—his junior! Truthfully, I have found that in many instances where an age gap this vast (twenty years or more) exists between a man and his younger bride, the woman is robbed of much of her youth and vitality. While such thievery may not ever be intentional on the part of the husband, the loss of vibrancy and zestfulness is often a considerable one for the much younger wife, all the same.

Ladies' Man

However, my most serious concern was that Rich had been making efforts to casually court several of these women at the same time. Apparently, he was not serious about a single one of them. Such two-timing (and three-, four-, and five-timing) behavior is a definite error for any gentleman of decency and integrity, not to mention a God-fearing man! Again, the womanizer's tricks would not be tolerated in the church I had been appointed by Almighty God to spearhead! Since this type of behavior went totally against the morals of godly character, it was my obligation as this brother's friend and pastor to call him to account for his inappropriate actions. And confront him I did.

To accomplish this task, I gathered all the people involved together in a private meeting, of which I was the mediator and judge. Adamant about his innocence, Rich initially denied the allegations of the young women, who accused him of harassment and inappropriate behavior. Actually, he did not blatantly contest the charges that he had invited them to dinner, engaged them in intimate conversation, visited their job sites, and unduly complimented them.

Instead, though Rich readily admitted to having a well-known flirtatious personality, this brother argued that in trying to involve himself with all of these young women as he had, his intentions had not been romantic ones! According to him, he had no personal interest in any of the young ladies he had made overtures to. Supposedly, his multiple exchanges with them had only been friendly gestures. He held that his suggestions of private get-togethers with each of these women were in no way indicative of any romantic interest or attraction on his part. To him, it was all casual interest and a general attempt to get to know these young women better. He even went so far as to actually question their rationale in thinking that he was trying to date any or all of them!

At this point in the process, I realized that Rich was not viewing the relationship dynamics between males and females realistically. I knew then he was not existing on a level of romantic maturity but was living in a realm of sheer fantasy!

Perhaps it is really true, after all, that age is nothing but a number. One would assume that, given his forty-three years, Rich would have had enough experience to know the realities and signals of courtship. Any time a man invites a woman whom he does not already know as a friend out to dinner for just the two of them; any time a man hands a woman his telephone number that is not on a business card or for the purpose of them discussing some professional matter together; and any time a man tells a woman that he finds her attractive and asks her personal questions about herself—any time he does these things, such initiatives will automatically—maybe even universally—be taken as romantic gestures! Even teenagers, maturing children who are just beginning to understand and participate in the workings of love and romance, generally know this much!

Any time a man invites a woman whom he does not already know as a friend out to dinner for just the two of them or tells a woman that he finds her attractive, such initiatives will be taken as romantic gestures!

I looked at Rich incredulously when he insisted that, all along, he had only been trying to be friendly and had not meant anything at all by his obvious flirting. I was forced to ask myself, "Is he lying, denying, or really just trying to be casual friends with all of these women? And how could he behave like this when everyone knows he is single and looking for a girlfriend or a wife, everyone knows he is a consummate flirt, and everyone apparently knows that this type of behavior is not new to him but is actually reflective of his reputation and recent past?" I had no answers, only suspicions.

Not wanting to be overly derogatory about my friend, brother, and parishioner, I have now accepted the fact that Rich was not living in reality where it concerned his relations with and actions toward the opposite sex. I reiterate that his mind-set about male/female interactions was one etched in fantasy, where single men are free to be openly suggestive to and flirtatious with single women, and no romantic notions are to be assumed or taken by the female receiving the advances and attention. Not only did he accept that distorted notion as fact, but in the warped recesses of this brother's mind, he also believed a single man could behave in a manner that clearly expressed his personal interest toward several females simultaneously!

In handling the situation, I rebuked Rich strongly for being out of order with his inappropriate behavior toward the women in the church. I even addressed this serious issue (without mentioning names, of course) publicly to the entire congregation, so that it might serve as a lesson for all. From this experience I have learned several lessons: Age does not guarantee wisdom or discretion; ignorance, whether feigned or real, causes individuals to act rather unwisely; and fantasy, when it becomes a stronghold, harms not only the individual but also everyone with whom the person comes in contact.

Brother Rich has now made the wise choice to mend his ways. At least, this is how things appear to be. Having made the proper apologies, he is now allowing himself to be steered by me, in the role of his concerned pastor and counselor, into a more respectful, gentlemanly view of females. He is learning that women are not poster girls to be looked upon for their physical attributes only, or creatures intended for the sole purpose of fulfilling men's needs and desires, or a predictable gender to be taken for granted and commonly lumped together in negative stereotypes. Neither are they the inferior half of mankind to be subdued and collected by superior-minded males!

Rather, Rich is learning what I myself have had to learn, sometimes the hard way: that every woman is a worthy being, specially crafted and designed by the Creator to birth and nurture humanity, to love and comfort one natural man, and to answer the divine call God has placed on her life. Moreover, since each woman is an individual, she is to be courted and romantically loved on an exclusive basis by one single man in her life, who is not to pursue others of her gender at the same time.

With man, it seems, the very idea of his being able to handle two (or more) women at one time is his biggest fantasy. But the notion that such is acceptable in the eyes of God, or even with society, is actually an intolerable and inexcusable fallacy.

7

You Can't Force Fruitfulness

Chapter Seven

You Can't Force Fruitfulness

The broad pattern for our lives, as planned and expressed by God from the very beginning of creation, is that we *"be fruitful and multiply"* (Genesis 1:28) in the context of sanctioned, healthy relationships. Ever since then, relationships, just like individuals, have produced fruit. Whether the resulting produce is good and nutritious or rotten and tainted is determined by the integrity and compatibility of the relationship and of the people involved.

According to the definition in *Webster's New Collegiate Dictionary,* the word *barren* means "not reproducing...not productive, producing little or no vegetation, desolate... unproductive of results or gain...devoid, lacking." Relationships can be barren. They can fail to produce good fruit, even when the affected parties expend long and arduous efforts to generate the desired results of fulfillment and happiness.

> Relationships can fail to produce good fruit, even when the affected parties expend long and arduous efforts.

These barren relationships are not pleasing to God, and they indicate that an improper relationship is being forced. This sort of situation can occur in a dating situation for many different reasons, which we will discuss in this chapter.

But I'm Lonely...

I often joke with the women in my congregation that they're so desperate for a man to end their loneliness that they don't even let one drop of water from his baptismal gown hit the floor before they claim him as their own and go after him. As soon as he's certifiably saved, they're on the chase. And the situation is often reversed as well, with men behaving much the same way, pursuing women who are not compatible with them just to avoid spending another Saturday night alone.

Is this sort of desperate pursuit of a mate what God intended? I don't think it is. This behavior is what gets people into barren relationships, where they know they're not completely compatible but are afraid that if they break up, they'll never find anyone else. Thus, they waste long stretches of their lives dating someone they know is not the one for them, perhaps even marrying this person, only to end up as alone as they felt they were in the beginning. The truth is, you can be just as alone when you're married as when you're single. Just having a mate won't help anything, but waiting for the right mate will.

Another thing: You're not lonely! You may be alone, but you're not lonely. Secular society teaches you that you're lonely and that you need a mate to be fulfilled. Movies and music preach romance and sex as the way to happiness, a way out of the mundane routine of life. But the Bible doesn't teach that. In fact, the Bible says some people will never get married and that being unmarried is sometimes the preferable state. For example, Paul advised the Corinthians not to get married because the times were so hard that it was easier not to be bound to anyone.

> *Now concerning virgins: I have no commandment from the Lord; yet I give judgment as one whom the Lord in His mercy has made trustworthy. I suppose therefore that this is good because of the present distress; that it is good for a man to remain as he is: Are you bound to a wife? Do not seek to be loosed. Are you loosed from a wife? Do not seek a wife. But even if you do marry, you have not sinned; and if a virgin marries, she has not sinned. Nevertheless such will have trouble in the flesh, but I would spare you.* (1 Corinthians 7:25–28)

Obviously, marriage is not necessary for happiness in life. What is necessary for happiness? Merely a knowledge of Jesus as your Savior and an understanding of His love for you.

> *We...rejoice in God through our Lord Jesus Christ, through whom we have now received the reconciliation.* (Romans 5:11)

So, go to the movies by yourself, hang out with yourself, enjoy yourself. Don't push a relationship with someone who is not compatible with you just because you're tired of being alone. If you can trust God for the air you breath and for the life you live, then you can trust Him to find your perfect mate. In the meantime, don't get stuck in a barren relationship.

Too Late to Leave Now

Another reason there are so many barren relationships is that once a person has committed a certain amount of time to a relationship, it becomes difficult to leave it.

A romance that has been going on for years is hard to leave. Time has been invested, and sometimes it's hard to break things off. The other person becomes a sort of habit for you, and so, despite the fact that the relationship is detrimental, you don't leave.

If you can trust God for the air you breath and for the life you live, then you can trust Him to find your perfect mate.

Also, one partner may feel that the other person has become extremely attached and is truly in love, and so he or she decides to stick with the relationship for the other's sake. Perhaps he thinks they can get by on one person's love. Or maybe she doesn't want to hurt him and is afraid of the confrontation that will be necessary to end the relationship.

Never a Good Idea

Whatever the reason, staying in a dating relationship with someone who is not compatible with you or who does not have the same goals as you is never a good idea. Even if your partner is completely in love with you, it is only a matter of time before he catches on that you are not so in love with him. Then you will not only have the breakup to deal with but your own dishonesty as well. Additionally, if you are truly in love with your partner but that love is unwise considering your partner's character or the nature of your relationship together, you are, again, only setting yourself up for disaster.

Don't waste your time in a fruitless relationship. Rely on God to help you find someone with whom you are truly compatible.

Compatible?

I've been throwing the word *compatible* around a lot, so let me explain what I mean by it and what it entails.

Webster's New Collegiate Dictionary defines compatible as "capable of existing together in harmony." This is an accurate definition, as far as it goes, but not a complete one. True compatibility in a romantic relationship involves much more. It involves complementing one another. Now, I don't mean *complimenting* as in saying, "Honey, you look beautiful in that dress" or "You're so smart and strong." I mean *complementing* one another's strengths and weaknesses. I mean one person making up for the weaknesses of the other and vice versa.

Compatibility also requires that you are heading in the same direction, that you have the same goals and interests. On a very basic level, this just means that you enjoy doing some of the same things. Perhaps both of you enjoy spending time outdoors, shopping, or relaxing in your home. It's important that you have somewhat the same idea of how you want to spend your time. Of course, if Mr. Right occasionally heads to the lake for some fishing while Miss Right goes to dinner with a girlfriend, that's probably healthy as well.

A deeper sense of heading in the same direction requires that you have the same long-term goals—that you both want kids or don't want kids, that you agree on where you should live, that you have similar beliefs, and that you believe you can help one another through life. It also requires that you both understand what your responsibilities will be if you get married. A woman with an MBA who is succeeding in the world should not have to support a lazy husband who won't get off the couch. Women, get a man who can provide for you! Men, do the same! Provide for one another equally and in your different ways.

It's Not a Race

Obviously, compatibility is not something we will find in everyone, or something we can manufacture or learn to live without. It's necessary and it's natural, so don't push it or pretend it's in your relationship when it isn't.

There is a reality television show called *Race to the Altar*. During the show, engaged couples compete in various challenges in order to be the first to make it to the altar and say their vows. Often Christian singles treat their dating relationships in a similar way. They know the ultimate goal is marriage, so they try to get to that point as soon as possible, as though they will get some special prize. Unfortunately, if they do not take the time to be sure they are making the correct decisions concerning their mate, all they will win is a broken heart and possibly a broken marriage.

Compatibility is not something we will find in everyone, or something we can manufacture or learn to live without.

Women are especially susceptible to this "racing" tendency. Perhaps this is because it is more socially acceptable to be a "bachelor" than it is to be an "old maid." Look, even just the different names we attribute to single men versus single women show the connotations that follow their marriage status. The word *bachelor* has a certain mystery and suaveness to it, while *old maid* implies that a single woman is ancient and dried out.

Like I said before, loneliness, or fear that the next one you date might be the last one, can cause us to act amazingly irrationally. In order to help the single ladies gauge whether they are in fact trying to race to the altar, I've included a list of three dating do nots. If you are engaging in the behaviors below, it might mean that you are pushing a bit too hard. These guidelines are especially for women, as men should take the leadership role in a relationship and occasionally violate these rules in order to move the relationship forward or be chivalrous.

1. **Don't be too aggressive, showing a much larger interest in your partner than he does in you.** Men become very uncomfortable when women are in hot pursuit and may even omit such women from those they consider potential mates. If he shows her any interest at all, she might be just his pastime when there's nothing more for him to do.

2. **Don't attempt to buy your partner's friendship and love by showering him with gifts.** This strategy, used by women to capture whomever they deem to be their true loves, usually ends with the woman being used and eventually discarded.

3. **Don't open up to or fall in love with him too soon.** No woman should open up to a man too soon. A lot of women, believe it or not, are in love with a man even before they've been introduced. A woman will fall in love with a man across the room because of the way he dresses, looks, or walks. If he can speak and handle himself well, she finds him irresistible. But whether he is really the man for her remains to be seen. Don't fall in love with someone you don't even know yet. Take the time to learn about one another.

Nothing New under the Sun

If you think incompatible, unsupportive couples are a creation of today's society, you're wrong. People have been joining themselves to the wrong mate throughout history. Let's take a look at some biblical examples of relationships gone wrong.

Job and His Wife (Job 1:1–2:10)

Job was a wealthy man who lived in Uz with his wife, three daughters, and seven sons. By all standards he was doing very well, and the Lord had blessed him because Job was faithful to Him. Unfortunately, Satan had identified him as a prime target.

In only one day, Satan took all Job's wealth, servants, and children. Then, when that did not sway Job's faith in the Lord, he also caused Job to be sick. Job's situation had been completely reversed. Every outward reason he had to praise God had been violently taken away. Yet Job's faith in God still remained steady. Not so with his wife.

Don't fall in love with someone you don't even know yet. Take the time to learn about one another.

Perhaps while times were good, Job's wife had been faithful to God and to Job, but when trials came, Job could not depend on her. She had nothing for him by way of support, but instead said, *"Do you still hold fast to your integrity? Curse God and die!"* (Job 2:9).

Job was righteous in his walk with the Lord, and his wife knew that. But that didn't stop her from blaming him, thinking that he must have somehow angered God, and thus caused all their troubles. It also didn't stop her from telling him to reject his God, cursing Him, and die. She advised Job to give up those things closest to him. She told him to give up his God and to give up his life.

For you men reading this book, it is my prayer that you will find a good woman to stand by you in trial and hardship, uplifting you and reminding you to trust in God.

Abigail and Nabal (1 Samuel 25)

Abigail and Nabal lived in the desert of Maon. They were very wealthy, with large stretches of land and many goats and sheep. The Bible is very specific as to their differences in character.

> *She was a woman of good understanding and beautiful appearance; but the man was harsh and evil in his doings. And he was of the house of Caleb.*
>
> (1 Samuel 25:3)

At this time David, the future king of Israel, was seeking refuge with his men. He heard that Nabal was nearby shearing sheep with his men and sent him a message.

> *David sent ten young men; and David said to the young men, "Go up to Carmel, go to Nabal, and greet him in my name. And thus you shall say to him who lives in prosperity: 'Peace be to you, peace to your house, and peace to all that you have! Now I have heard that you have shearers. Your shepherds were with us, and we did not hurt them, nor was there anything missing from them all the while they were in Carmel. Ask your young men, and they will tell you. Therefore let my young men find favor in your eyes, for we come on a feast day. Please give whatever comes to your hand to your servants and to your son David.'"* (verses 5–8)

True to his mean and foolish character, Nabal did not respond to this message by reciprocating David's respectful manner or by acting according to the accepted rules of hospitality. He refused to help David and his men although they had treated his men well. As a result, he incurred David's wrath. David swore to kill him and every man in his household. But not everyone in Nabal's household was so foolhardy. When a servant told Abigail what was happening, she took action.

> *Abigail made haste and took two hundred loaves of bread, two skins of wine, five sheep already dressed, five seahs of roasted grain, one hundred clusters of raisins, and two hundred cakes of figs, and loaded them on donkeys. And she said to her servants, "Go on before me; see, I am coming after you." But she did not tell her husband Nabal. So it was, as she rode on the donkey, that she went down under cover of the hill; and there were David and his men, coming down toward her, and she met them.* (1 Samuel 25:18–20)

Abigail intercepted David just as he and his men were about to attack her household because of Nabal's rude behavior. She fell at his feet and said the following.

> *On me, my lord, on me let this iniquity be! And please let your maidservant speak in your ears, and hear the words of your maidservant. Please, let not my lord regard this scoundrel Nabal. For as his name is, so is he: Nabal is his name, and folly is with him. But I, your maidservant, did not see the young men of my lord whom you sent. Now therefore, my lord, as the LORD lives and as your soul lives, since the LORD has held you back from coming to bloodshed and from avenging yourself with your own hand, now then, let your enemies and those who seek harm for my lord be as Nabal. And now this present which your maidservant*

*has brought to my lord, let it be given to the young men
who follow my lord.* (1 Samuel 25:24–27)

Not only did Abigail humble herself, but she also went
on to prophesy concerning David's eventual victory over
his enemies. As a result, David spared Nabal and all of his
household, thanking God for sending Abigail to him.

One of the greatest mistakes you can make is to join
yourself to someone who's going a different direction than you
are, or worse, going nowhere at all.

Thus, though Nabal would have destroyed his household's wealth and caused their death with his foolishness,
Abigail's wisdom saved them all. While it is wonderful that
she was able to do this, it is a shame that she had to. Nabal
was obviously not a fitting counterpart for such a wise, kind,
and beautiful woman. From the verses above, we can tell
that he was not someone she could trust or respect—two of
the most important ingredients in a good marriage!

Don't Be Another Example

Want to keep from joining the list of Abigails and Jobs?
Here are some little tests and checks that will help you determine if your relationship is headed in the right direction.

Five Ways to Know If a Potential Mate Is Compatible

1. **His or her goals and aspirations align with
   your goals for the future.** One of the greatest

mistakes you can make is to join yourself to some-one who's going a different direction than you are, or worse, going nowhere at all.

2. **You feel comfort in the presence of the indi-vidual rather than negative anxiety.**

3. **The majority of your time together is not spent in conflict nor in total agreement.** You shouldn't be always arguing or always agreeing—always tear-ing each other's hair out or always kissing. Court-ship should include a certain amount of balance. You are each individuals, so it is inevitable that you will sometimes disagree and argue. If you never argue, then perhaps one of you is making too many conces-sions or maybe neither of you has as much invested as you previously thought. After all, never fighting often implies a complete lack of interest, not undy-ing love.

   However, arguing all the time is no way to live either. You should have an effective manner of conflict reso-lution that allows each of you to voice your opinions and then come to some sort of decision or compro-mise.

4. **He or she does not pressure you to do things that go against your moral judgment.** If some-one pushes you to do things you have previously stated you will not do, that implies a lack of respect. I'm not only referring to someone pushing you to go further then you had intended physically. If a person encourages you to disobey the rules of your house-hold, then that is also a lack of respect. If you are

younger and have a curfew, but the person you are with consistently asks you break it, disappointing your family, that is disrespect. Someone who disrespects your family and disrespects you in this way will only continue in this path.

5. **You are able to resolve conflicts in a healthy manner without your mate shutting down or blowing up.** Conflicts and disagreements are going to happen, but when they do, can you and your mate work through them? You need to be able to converse with one another in a productive way that neither involves always yelling and getting out of control nor ignoring the problem and refusing to talk about it. Remember, you're supposed to be a team. So if you can't make decisions as a team, even hard ones, something is wrong.

Ten Things to Know about an Abusive Man

1. He uses Scripture to force his mate into submission.

2. He alienates her from friends and family.

3. He constantly belittles her instead of encouraging her to excel.

4. He's jealous of her and embarrasses her in public.

5. He showers her with gifts after physically or verbally abusing her.

6. He refuses to be confronted by his mate.

7. He casts blame for every negative situation on his mate.

8. He tries to control her decisions and actions.

9. His mate's family and friends do not like him and advise her to discontinue the relationship.

10. He must know where she is at all times. He keeps tabs on her day and night through e-mail, cell phone calls, etc.

Eight Things to Know about a Controlling Woman

1. She has many insecurities, which she expects him to alleviate continually.

2. She tries to buy his friendship or love by showering him with gifts.

3. She alienates him from his friends and family.

4. She uses tricks to control him. (For example, at a party where no one is paying attention to her she may fake a stomachache so that her mate must leave to take her home, thus ensuring that his attention is on her.)

5. She can't talk about sensitive issues without arguing.

6. She doesn't allow him to make decisions for himself.

7. Her mate's family and friends do not like her and advise him to discontinue the relationship.

8. She uses her looks and physical intimacy to get her way.

Spot Potential Problems

Listed here are eight statements. Read each one and check whether you agree or disagree with each statement as it pertains to your relationship.

1. We can talk about anything openly and honestly.
   __Agree __Disagree

2. I am satisfied with the amount of affection between my partner and me.

   __Agree __Disagree

3. My partner helps to build my self-esteem.

   __Agree __Disagree

4. We joke and laugh together.

   __Agree __Disagree

5. We don't have large disputes concerning financial matters.

   __Agree __Disagree

6. I know my partner will be an excellent parent.

   __Agree __Disagree

7. We are not overly irritated or disgusted by one another's habits or quirks.

   __Agree __Disagree

8. We are able to share in making decisions.

   __Agree __Disagree

Take a look at the questions you answered "disagree" to. Are there a lot of them? Are they things that can be worked on? Hopefully this has given you more of a guideline to gauge your relationships by.

Don't forget, also, that parents and friends can be a great gauge of relationship compatibility. If everyone around you thinks you're going wrong, maybe they have a point. Talk to your friends and ask them to tell you honestly if you ever date someone who is not compatible with you. Having opened the door for honesty, perhaps they will be more forward about pointing out any potential problems.

Remember also that a good relationship always brings the couple closer to God, not further away. If your partner isn't encouraging you to grow in your faith, if you're not praying and gaining more godly wisdom together, then that's a sure sign your relationship is not pleasing to Him.

In everything, ask God for wisdom and He will guide you. You just have to listen.

Right Person,
Wrong Love

8

Chapter Eight

Right Person, Wrong Love

Possibly, you have already cleared out all of these unhealthy relationships, including those forbidden relationships that once attracted you so much. And, maybe, your relationship problem may seem minor in comparison to the ones previously discussed. Quite possibly, you are involved in an honorable, God-sanctioned marriage, but the connection with your partner seems to have soured. The warm intimacy you once shared has turned into cold detachment. Your marriage feels like it is on the rocks instead of being built on the Rock.

Maybe you feel stuck in a lousy situation and just have no idea what to do about it anymore. You once promised before God to love, honor, and cherish your mate "until death do us part," and you have no intention of going back on your vow of lifelong fidelity, even if it kills you. But, if you are really honest, deep down inside lurks the nagging desire for a way out of this no-win situation in which you are trapped. You may have even secretly wished that your spouse would go out and commit adultery just so you would have biblical justification to file for divorce!

If you act according to His rules, God will meet you right in the midst of your intense conflict and negotiate a lasting peace.

Hold on! Don't give up yet! There is a solution, other than a sin-ridden choice that could lead to even more disaster than you are in right now. I want to give you renewed hope that your heavenly Father will not leave you stranded in a loveless union, and so I am praying this for you:

Now may the God of hope fill you with all joy and peace in believing, that you may abound in hope by the power of the Holy Spirit. (Romans 15:13)

I know that just now your spouse may seem to be your enemy because you are at such odds with one another. Although your home was once peaceful and serene, it has become the battlefront for your personal war. If you are willing to act according to His rules, however, God will meet you right in the midst of your intense conflict and negotiate a lasting peace.

> *When a man's ways please the LORD, He makes even his enemies to be at peace with him.* (Proverbs 16:7)

When you begin to act in faith and do what God wants you to do, He will step in and accomplish what you cannot. You may feel as if your marriage is impossible to heal, but our Lord is the God of the impossible. If He could reconcile the absolute hostility between the Jews and the Gentiles and unite them together through His Son's death on the cross, I am certain that He is able to bring peace and wholeness to your fractionalized marriage. As you read the following Scripture passage, personalize it with your name and the name of your spouse, and accept it as a promise for the future of your marital relationship:

> *For He Himself is our peace, who has made both* [husband and wife] *one, and has broken down the middle wall of separation, having abolished in His flesh the enmity,....so as to create in Himself one new man* [and union] *from the two, thus making peace, and that He might reconcile them both to God in one body through the cross, thereby putting to death the enmity. And He came and preached peace to you who were afar off and to those who were near.* (Ephesians 2:14–17)

As you read on, you will learn some of the things you can do to fix your faltering relationship or simply to improve and fix up a slightly faulty one. Remember, God calls us to put our best foot forward when it comes to relationships.

> *If it is possible, as much as depends on you, live peaceably with all men.* (Romans 12:18)

This includes your mate. Just keep in mind that God only requires you to do what you are capable of doing. He never asks you to change your mate or do the impossible—that's His job.

Different Sometimes Means Difficult

Integral to the process of perfecting our intimate relationships is a willingness on all of our parts to be open and honest about ourselves. As men and women, males and females, members of opposite sexes, two separate genders, we have to be truthful enough with ourselves to define, acknowledge, and know first who we are as individuals and then who we are as partners in our interplay with our respective mates. We need to know our similarities, our differences, and the ways in which we interact with one another. Only when God's people begin to shamelessly accept and seriously address who we are in entirety, fully embracing both our spiritual and natural realities, will we be able to learn the ways in which we can properly deal with and relate to one another as preordained, predetermined, and predesigned by our Creator.

Separate but Equal

In spite of what liberal laws, certain progressive movements, and some scientific studies tell us, we must first accept the obvious truth that men and women significantly differ in many respects. Unquestionably, we are very similar to one another, as well—mostly in a general human way. The fact remains, however, that males and females are separate, sometimes opposing, and often contrasting genders. As such, we have distinct behaviors, roles, responsibilities, and purposes, according to the original intention of God. God was the first one, in fact, to assign gender roles. God made Eve as a helper for Adam, who was meant to work and care for the garden. (See Genesis 2:15–24.) God further distinguished the gender differences in Genesis chapter three.

> *To the woman He said: "I will greatly multiply your sorrow and your conception; in pain you shall bring forth children; your desire shall be for your husband, and he shall rule over you." Then to Adam He said, "Because you have heeded the voice of your wife, and have eaten from the tree of which I commanded you, saying, 'You shall not eat of it': cursed is the ground for your sake; in toil you shall eat of it all the days of your life. Both thorns and thistles it shall bring forth for you, and you shall eat the herb of the field. In the sweat of your face you shall eat bread till you return to the ground, for out of it you were taken; for dust you are, and to dust you shall return."* (Genesis 3:16–19)

The fact is that males and females are separate, sometimes opposing, and often contrasting genders.

Our differences as men and women, it seems, are the crux of the mystery of why we come together as naturally and easily as we do—when we do—in the first place.

> *There be three things which are too wonderful for me, yea, four which I know not: The way of an eagle in the air; the way of a serpent upon a rock; the way of a ship*

in the midst of the sea; and the way of a man with a maid. (Proverbs 30:18–19 KJV)

Yet, even in our successful pairings, we are ever reminded of the distinctiveness of our gender perspectives. With all the problems, discrepancies, and potent misunderstandings that inevitably surface between us, sometimes we become detached from the very people we once claimed to have loved so fiercely.

But even if you do marry, you have not sinned; and if a virgin marries, she has not sinned. Nevertheless such will have trouble in the flesh, but I would spare you.
(1 Corinthians 7:28)

Before the predictable contrasts build to the point of becoming "irreconcilable differences" and permanently separate a God-fearing couple, an accurate assessment of gender roles and tendencies as well as common marital mistakes is needed.

Social Differences

Not only are we made differently, but society continues the trend. For example, females are traditionally taught to be sweet, loving, and compassionate. From birth, their lives are permeated with this tenderness of heart and spirit: from the soft pastel colors of their clothing, the lace that lines their cribs, and the cuddling they receive and are encouraged to reciprocate, young women are nurtured to be nurturers. By the time a girl is a year old, she has been given her first baby doll, with which she practices her mothering skills. By the age of three, she receives a Barbie doll, which sends an equally feminine—though somewhat different—message, making her subconsciously aware of her womanhood and sexuality.

On the other hand, young boys are given trucks, baseball bats, jerseys, footballs, hockey pucks, and GI Joe dolls, all of which help to shape and reinforce their masculinity. Even beyond masculinity, young boys are taught the art of being macho—they are to be men who dominate. Boys learn early that it is manly to conquer and control whatever is immediately at hand, without considering the consequences, and to win at all costs.

Thus, the behaviors and attitudes a young man is taught are generally the direct opposites of those taught to a young woman. He is rough, while she is soft. Where she cuddles, he wrestles. She is taught to consider her future, while he learns to think in terms of the present. Where verbal expression and communication are concerned, the girl is often encouraged to become extroverted, and the boy, more introverted.

The Apple Doesn't Fall Far from the Tree

In addition to behavior learned from society, family upbringing can have a large impact on how a person perceives relationships and acts in them.

Impaired marriages can be a generational trend, resulting from faulty modeling. What children see acted out in front of them in their homes and what they are taught—the subliminal and blatant messages that are passed down to them—can affect their future relationships as well as their personalities.

For example, in the neighborhood where I grew up, a young woman gave birth to a baby girl. By the time this baby girl was nine months old, her mother was pregnant again. This second baby, also a girl, was born when the first girl was only eighteen months old. An additional nine months later, the young woman became pregnant again. By the birth of the third baby, the oldest child was only twenty-seven months old, but she was needed by Mom for assistance with the new infant. So, the young mother sat her oldest child on the sofa, handed her the newborn baby (propped up with a pillow for support), and had the twenty-seven-month-old toddler feed her youngest sibling. Hence, the oldest daughter received her instructions in motherhood before she had truly begun the experience of childhood.

Family upbringing can have a large impact on how a person perceives relationships and acts in them.

Understandably, by the time this oldest child was barely eighteen, she was ready to leave her mother's household and find a man to care for her. Soon after, she met a young man her age who was the youngest child in his family. As such, the idea and expectation that he himself was always to be cared for and catered to was inbred in the young man's nature and character, because his particular birth order had made him accustomed to being doted on. The two young people decided to come together, both secretly hoping to get their needs met through the other. However, because these two immature eighteen-year-olds were seeking the same things from each other—care and provision—their union was troubled and unbalanced, since both wanted to receive and neither was truly capable or prepared to give.

I Love You...I Love You Not

Given all the various ways that men and women are different from one another, it's only natural that two such hugely separate people endeavoring to become one is not always an easy undertaking. Sometimes it may seem completely unfeasible.

In the ups, downs, and U-turns of marriage I hear opposites: I love you/I hate you; get out of my face/come near me; I need you/I don't need you. God, through the covenant of marriage, is asking you to give up who you are and come together with one mind and one flesh, but at the same time He is expecting you to have individuality. He wants you to be yourself yet so close to your mate that you can finish any sentence he or she starts. You know when your mate is happy or sad. You know when he or she is making a bad choice. You know what's going to get on your mate's nerves before they even come to it.

What's the way to get this close to your spouse? What's the way to learn this type of intimacy? First of all, only God can provide the power you need to love your mate wholly and unconditionally; this type of intimacy is a tall order for a mere human. You must love and provide for your spouse, making his or her needs your own. This is one of the main problems in marriage today: The two have not become one because each person is looking out only for himself or herself. If you are each looking out for one another's needs wholeheartedly, then you will both have your needs met.

Man, Provide for Your Woman

God intended husbands to provide for their wives. They are to provide not only monetarily and physically, but also emotionally. They are to build their wives up at the same time they are building a home.

Providing for your wife shows her that you love her and are concerned for her welfare. You must consider whether you are capable of providing for a woman at that level before you get married.

Only God can provide the power you need to love your mate wholly and unconditionally.

When my wife, Jeannie, and I were first starting out, I took her to an apartment—our new home. The building was falling apart and the area was notorious for its prostitutes and drugs. I told her it was temporary; we were just going to stay there until we got things together. She said, "You stay here. I'm going to my mother's house." She knew I was not providing a good home for her. She also knew about my past with drugs and that this was the last place I should be staying. I thank God that she didn't agree to stay in that home. We ended up getting a different apartment. It was old but in a nice area. The rent was $117.50 a month, which was more than I could afford. But the church next door owned the apartment, so I paid for it by cleaning the church every night after work. It was hard, but I provided for my family.

In Genesis, we find a scriptural account of what happens when a man fails to live up to the responsibility God has placed upon him. As you read this story, remember that the God-ordained custom in those days was that when a man died, leaving his wife a childless widow, his brother was to marry the widow and sire a male heir, who could then inherit the dead man's share of the family fortune and provide for his widowed mother.

Judah had three sons: Er, Onan, and Shelah. When the oldest son, Er, had grown, Judah found a wife for him named Tamar. But, because Er was wicked, the Lord caused him to die and Tamar was left a widow. In keeping with the provision for widows, Tamar was given to Er's brother Onan as his wife. But he did not provide for her as a husband should. Here's what happened.

> *Judah said to Onan, "Go in to your brother's wife and marry her, and raise up an heir to your brother." But Onan knew that the heir would not be his; and it came to pass, when he went in to his brother's wife, that he emitted on the ground, lest he should give an heir to his brother. And the thing which he did displeased the LORD; therefore He killed him also.* (Genesis 38:8–10)

Onan refused to produce an heir for his brother, thereby refusing to provide for Tamar, and so God struck him down. Now, Judah still had another son, Shelah, who should be given to Tamar. Let's see what happens.

Then Judah said to Tamar his daughter-in-law, "Remain a widow in your father's house till my son Shelah is grown." For he said, "Lest he also die like his brothers." And Tamar went and dwelt in her father's house. Now in the process of time the daughter of Shua, Judah's wife, died; and Judah was comforted, and went up to his sheepshearers at Timnah, he and his friend Hirah the Adullamite. And it was told Tamar, saying, "Look, your father-in-law is going up to Timnah to shear his sheep." So she took off her widow's garments, covered herself with a veil and wrapped herself, and sat in an open place which was on the way to Timnah; for she saw that Shelah was grown, and she was not given to him as a wife.

(Genesis 38:11–14)

Judah sent Tamar to her father's house, even though the custom of the time required that she stay in his household. He did not want to give Tamar to his last son, Shelah, because he was afraid that he, too, would die. And so, Tamar was forced to take matters into her own hands in a desperate manner.

When Judah saw her, he thought she was a harlot, because she had covered her face. Then he turned to her by the way, and said, "Please let me come in to you"; for he did not know that she was his daughter-in-law. So she said, "What will you give me, that you may come in to me?" And he said, "I will send a young goat from the flock." So she said, "Will you give me a pledge till you send it?" Then he said, "What pledge shall I give you?" So she said, "Your signet and cord, and your staff that is in your hand." Then he gave them to her, and went in to her, and she conceived by him. (verses 15–18)

Tamar finally had the heir Onan had deprived her of, but it was only by pretending to be a prostitute that she forced Judah to do right by her.

> *So she arose and went away, and laid aside her veil and put on the garments of her widowhood. And Judah sent the young goat by the hand of his friend the Adullamite, to receive his pledge from the woman's hand, but he did not find her. Then he asked the men of that place, saying, "Where is the harlot who was openly by the roadside?" And they said, "There was no harlot in this place." So he returned to Judah and said, "I cannot find her. Also, the men of the place said there was no harlot in this place." Then Judah said, "Let her take them for herself, lest we be shamed; for I sent this young goat and you have not found her." And it came to pass, about three months after, that Judah was told, saying, "Tamar your daughter-in-law has played the harlot; furthermore she is with child by harlotry." So Judah said, "Bring her out and let her be burned!" When she was brought out, she sent to her father-in-law, saying, "By the man to whom these belong, I am with child." And she said, "Please determine whose these are; the signet and cord, and staff." So Judah acknowledged them and said, "She has been more righteous than I, because I did not give her to Shelah my son." And he never knew her again.* (Genesis 39:19–26)

Onan, whose name most fittingly means "my iniquity," selfishly chose to spill his seed on the ground instead of fathering an heir with Tamar, causing her to remain childless and without an inheritance. Thus, she had no permanent covering. God was angered at Onan's perversion, and like his brother before him, God slew Onan because of his wickedness. As the patriarch of the family, Judah was equally guilty for not attending to the necessary provision for Tamar.

The lesson of this story is this: When men are not real men, when they are not the covering for their wives that God intends them to be, they waste their seed and destroy their women.

Woman, Provide for Your Man

Women are not the only halves of romantic relationships who sometimes need extra attention and caretaking, however. Indeed, it is often the case that a relatively good man will require the specialized love, patience, and attention of his wife so that the ragged, imperfect areas of his flawed character might be pruned from him. This qualifies him as a diamond-in-the-rough—or better still, as a potential-laden tree that needs individualized pruning so that it might begin to bear healthy, desirable fruit!

If a man is a tree, the earth in which he is planted and the soil from which he receives nourishment for growth is the home environment created by the women with whom he has had relationships.

When men are involved in multiple relationships, they are grown in the fields of different women. As a result, when they do finally find their permanent mates, they are often not totally what their wives need and desire. When a man comes from the unhealthy, lacking, or stripped soil of another female, a woman sometimes has to replant her man in her own soil and fertilize him with the nutrients and minerals of her particular choosing because he is now hers.

The man is the fig tree that needs to be dug out of its corrupt soil of the past, fertilized, and given the proper growth supplements after replanting. His wife is the compassionate, forgiving gardener, intent on seeing him grow and bear good fruit. (See Luke 13:6–9.) She takes on the challenging role of becoming his loyal, faithful caretaker.

If a man is a tree, the soil from which he receives nourishment is the home environment created by the women with whom he has had relationships.

The fact of the matter is that, sometimes, when a man appears to be absolutely rotten, he actually has great potential to become very good. Often a man who is bad is really not so bad that he has to be permanently discarded or thrown away. Sometimes, if the undesirable aspects of his personality, attitudes, and behaviors were to be carefully cut away and discarded by a wife who recognized his promise, he would turn out to be a truly healthy and pleasant tree. If the crooked, immature, diseased, or unyielding trees are nurtured by women who really care, and they are replanted in richer soil, the fruit they yield might be surprisingly good and satisfying.

The woman, being the gardener, has compassion on this less-than-ideal tree who is her man. She stands up for the tree. She determines to dig her man up from the corrupt soil of his former girlfriends, pull up his shallow roots, eliminate the corruption and improper influences of his former environment, fertilize him with her undy-ing love and devotion, shelter him through the storms and inclement weather of life, nurture him with her faith and support, stick with him through the trials and tests of the relationship, believe in him amid all the turbulence, stabilize him with the restrictive guide-wires of her personal standards, and nurse him back to emotional and psychological health.

Scripture gives an example of a godly woman who provides for her family and husband in Proverbs.

Who can find a virtuous wife? For her worth is far above rubies. The heart of her husband safely trusts her; so he will have no lack of gain. She does him good and not evil all the days of her life. She seeks wool and flax, and willingly works with her hands. She is like the merchant ships, she brings her food from afar. She also rises while it is yet night, and provides food for her household, and a portion for her maidservants. She considers a field and buys it; from her profits she plants a vineyard. She girds herself with strength, and strengthens her arms. She perceives that her merchandise is good, and her lamp does not go out by night. She stretches out her hands to the distaff, and her hand holds the spindle. She extends her hand to the poor, yes, she reaches out her hands to the needy. She is not afraid of snow for her household, for all her household is clothed with scarlet. She makes tapestry for herself; her clothing is fine linen and purple. Her husband is known in the gates, when he sits among the elders of the land. She makes linen garments and sells them, and supplies sashes for the merchants. Strength and honor are her clothing; she shall rejoice in time to come. She opens her mouth with wisdom, and on her tongue is the law of kindness. She watches over the ways of her household, and does not eat the bread of idleness. Her children rise up and call her blessed; her husband also, and he praises her.

(Proverbs 31:10–28)

It is when husbands and wives provide for one another that they grow close to one another. When they give up thinking of themselves and begin thinking only of one another, their souls intertwine. However, not all marital problems stem out of failing to nurture and provide for one another.

Still Unequally Yoked?

As we discussed earlier, Scripture says, *"Do not be unequally yoked together with unbelievers"* (2 Corinthians 6:14). Unfortunately, when reading this Scripture, we tend to focus only on the word *"unbelievers."* The fact of the matter is that while you may both be believers, you might still be *"unequally yoked."*

It is when husbands and wives provide for one another that they grow close to one another.

Just as the farmer's yoke was not properly constructed to distribute the workload between the two animals, given the individual strengths and weakness of each, so the yoke of the marriage bond can develop in such a way as to distort the balance of power between husband and wife. I have observed over the years that certain dysfunctional behavioral patterns can form between husbands and wives that hinder the growth of their intimacy and prevent the production of good fruit. These problems are not impossible to correct, but the first step is recognizing there are problems. Read the list below with an open heart, searching your own marriage relationship for any weaknesses or signs that one or more of these problems might apply to you.

Too Much or Not Enough Communication

When one member of a couple talks too much or when a spouse does not talk enough, the wrong messages are inevitably sent. In the former case, when the communication is excessive, it is quite often the female doing the talking, sometimes giving her husband the impression that she is a "know-it-all." Eventually, his tendency will be to tune out all her chatter because he thinks none of it has any relevance. On the other hand, when a husband tends to withhold communication and conversation, his wife interprets his silence as evidence of a "problem" that he doesn't want to talk about.

Men must understand that women tend to have a reservoir of emotions and experiences from their past, which they draw from for the present. Similar to the ebb and flow of water, women are known to generate and regenerate communication. Husbands must be careful not to fault their wives for their constant communicating; it is their nature. At the same time, men can learn to be more expressive and verbal, especially when there is a serious need for discussion. However, the intelligent woman who understands that the man's natural tendency is to be reserved in conversation will not attempt to push him out of character by insisting that he "just talk about it."

Confessing Your Past to Your Mate

When confession of past sins is being made, it is important that the right individual hear the disclosure. This is not always your spouse, even when the confession concerns your relationship. Remember, issues of the past that have already been confessed to God and covered by the blood of Jesus do not necessarily need to be retrieved from the Sea of Forgetfulness and shared with your mate! Sometimes, your spouse is not prepared to hear the whole, unvarnished truth about your past.

Many successful marriages have been destroyed through the encouragement of spiritual leaders and others who promote untimely disclosure. I happen to know of a particular marriage that crumbled, even though the couple was at the peak of marital happiness, because a traveling minister strongly encouraged the seminar attendees to "confess all" to their mates. Upon hearing this advice, the husband revealed to his wife that he had engaged in an affair many years previously, while she was pregnant with their first child. His wife was absolutely brokenhearted and devastated by his admission, to the extent that she could no longer continue in the marriage. Indeed, having the affair was absolutely wrong on the husband's part. However, had this man admitted his sin and truly repented only to God, accepted the Lord's forgiveness and cleansing, and not heeded such unspiritual advice, this once happy couple might still be married today.

If this man had felt the need to confess to someone, his best option would have been to seek out counseling with his pastor or another mature, trustworthy, spiritual leader in his own church. In doing so, he would have established an ongoing relationship with another man who could have guided him wisely, based on personal knowledge of the whole situation, and who could have held him accountable for his subsequent behavior.

Be mindful, dear reader, that in saying this, I am not advocating dishonesty or concealment. Rather, I am recommending that you use prudence when sharing the unseemly things of your past with your spouse. You need to know both your mate and the nature of your relationship so well that you can determine whether confession will indeed end up being good for your soul.

Comparing Your Mate with Others

If you like the idea of continually being in hot water with your mate, just make comparing your mate with others a regular habit. Almost universally, women seem to be highly offended by this tendency in their men. Gentlemen, do not compare your wife with another woman. She wants you to be in love with her own unique qualities and individuality, not how she stacks up next to someone else, or even how something about her reminds you of another woman. She prides herself on being a Designer Original, so treat her as such. Ladies, the same is true concerning your husbands. Do not compare your mate with a previous man in your life—unless, of course, you are telling him how much better he is!

Dwelling on Your Partner's Weaknesses

For most of us, our sensitive spots are closely tied to our weaknesses. Pointing out another's faults and flaws not only produces hurt feelings, but it also makes you appear insensitive and arrogant, even if your only intention is to help. Getting others to address what you see as their shortcomings requires a delicate touch.

> *But speaking the truth in love, we are to grow up in all aspects into Him, who is the head, even Christ.*
> (Ephesians 4:15 NAS)

Self-esteem, self-worth, and personal security are all built up and strengthened by emphasizing a person's positive characteristics. Dwelling on the individual's negative attributes can tear the positive ones down.

> *Therefore let us pursue the things which make for peace and the things by which one may edify* [or, build up] *another.* (Romans 14:19)

> *Therefore encourage one another, and build up one another....Esteem them very highly in love....Live in peace with one another.*
> (1 Thessalonians 5:11, 13 NAS)

In summary, the philosophy that says showing others their weaknesses makes them stronger is, more often than not, false. Emphasis on weaknesses makes one weaker, is not encouraging, and definitely does not build the other up. Since the marriage relationship is about strengthening and esteeming our mates, we should focus on the positive aspects of our partners to help make them stronger.

Allowing Outsiders to Meddle in the Marriage

The Bible tells us, *"What God has joined together, let not man separate"* (Mark 10:9). Here, God is speaking about the actual institution of marriage as a covenant to be respected by those inside and outside of it. The marriage is set apart unto itself as a separate unit with its own identity. It does not include parents, children, friends, or even church leaders. Manipulation of the marital relationship by anyone outside of the union must not be tolerated, even if it comes from a well-meaning pastor or Christian counselor.

Clinging to Your Parents instead of Your Spouse

Therefore shall a man leave his father and his mother, and shall cleave unto his wife: and they shall be one flesh. (Genesis 2:24 KJV)

The philosophy that says showing others their weaknesses makes them stronger is, more often than not, false.

Parents often remain tied to their married children through an emotional umbilical cord long after the physical one has been cut. Parents' unsolicited involvement in their married children's lives is a subtle form of witchcraft, which needs to be broken through the power of the blood of Jesus.

On the other hand, adult children have often not grown up emotionally and financially and declared their independence from Mom and Dad by assuming the full responsibilities of adulthood. Frequently, it has been too easy for some to remain dependent on their parents rather than take on the burdens of supporting and making decisions for themselves. Such juvenile adults, however, pay a high price for remaining dependent: They have to surrender much of the control of their lives to their parents. When people like this get married, inevitably their opposite-sex parent has more influence over them than their mate does. This causes friction in the marriage because it injures the spouse's place as mate.

Sharing Intimate Information with Outsiders

We must be extremely careful of what we share about our marriages with people outside of our unions. Not only are the intimate details of our particular bonds none of their business, but quite often we are first turning to outside friends for consolation and support when we should be addressing any problem situations with our mates. Wives are often more guilty of actually committing this offense, but husbands share part of the responsibility when they fail to keep the lines of communication open or fail to really listen to what their wives say.

Apologizing Later instead of First Getting Permission

The false assumption that sacrifice afterward is better than consideration and obedience in the first place (1 Samuel 15:22) is the basic fallacy behind a major problem in too many marriages today. This hindrance creates very serious strife in a marriage—not *may* create or *possibly* creates or *might* create but *absolutely* creates division! Too many husbands have the idea that they can do whatever they want to do whenever they want to do it, as long as later, when the time of reckoning comes, they buy their wives dinner or a dress or produce some other type of bribe to make peace. However, the end result is quite tragic when that "last straw" act of the husband occurs and breaks his wife's patience and spirit! Unknown to the man, the woman has in her storehouse of memories his track record of offenses. When she is finally destroyed by his last affront to her dignity, she will realize that all his former apologies—and gifts!—were insincere.

The moral of the story, then, is get permission, or it will cost you the money in your pocket and the peace in your relationship!

Projecting a False Character

Unfortunately, in many cases, the church has forced us as Christians to try to be who we are not. "Spiritual cloning" happens when a leading figure from the outside or a dominating personality within a church attracts others through charisma, authority, or allure. When weaker personalities attempt to mimic the outstanding person, they lose their own individuality and uniqueness. Taking on that person's character traits and personality, these envious people start to dress like, think like, talk like, worship like, and laugh like the dominant personality—even taking on that person's peculiar mannerisms. Of course, they carry home this facade, projecting a false character to their mates.

Institutions and industries other than the church that produce clones include the media, fashion, and Wall Street (the rat race). In times of crisis, however, when the storms of life are raging within relationships, the false character never fails to drop off, revealing the true individual behind the facade. This explosive situation has the potential of sparking disaster. Remember, who you are in the midst of the storm is who you really are.

Making Your Children the Focus of the Marriage

It is necessary to emphasize that children are a part of the family but not a part of the marriage. Because a mother is generally the main source of care and nurture for her children, especially the younger and more dependent they are on her, she is particularly prone to neglecting her husband while tending to the offspring. She will often forego her first duty to the marriage and the meeting of her husband's needs for their sakes. However, since the marital union was hopefully established before the children came along, her husband has proprietary rights to her focus and attention. When a woman allows her children to take up all of her time and energy, they usurp her husband's rightful place with her.

Because a mother is generally the main source of care and nurture for her children, especially the younger and more dependent they are on her, she is particularly prone to neglecting her husband while tending to them.

Therefore, we must be careful that our children do not manipulate our marriage bonds. To prevent it from happening, make decisions together, and stick to them—no matter how upset the kids may become. It is also a good idea to schedule "dates" with your spouse—times when the two of you can have some time alone, whether it be at a fancy restaurant or in your living room, to reconnect and reaffirm your relationship.

The Real Formula

Although the above list of faulty behaviors is by no means all-inclusive, the avoidance of these hindrances alone could go a long way to strengthen your marriage. However, when we humans try to change our behavior and we stop doing something we know is detrimental for us, we are predisposed to replace one bad habit with another. I suggest that, in your attempts to fix the flaws in your marriage, you substitute God's design and follow His instructions for positive marital behavior:

> *Submitting to one another in the fear of God. Wives, submit to your own husbands, as to the Lord. For the husband is head of the wife, as also Christ is head of the church; and He is the Savior of the body. Therefore, just as the church is subject to Christ, so let the wives be to their own husbands in everything. Husbands, love your wives, just as Christ also loved the church and gave Himself for her, that He might sanctify and cleanse her with the washing of water by the word, that He might present her to Himself a glorious church, not having spot or wrinkle or any such thing, but that she should be holy and without blemish. So husbands ought to love their own wives as their own bodies; he who loves his wife loves himself. For no one ever hated his own flesh, but nourishes and cherishes it, just as the Lord does the church. For we are members of His body, of His flesh and of His bones. "For this reason a man shall leave his father and mother and be joined to his wife, and the two shall*

become one flesh."...Nevertheless let each one of you in particular so love his own wife as himself, and let the wife see that she respects her husband.

(Ephesians 5:21–31, 33)

What a formula for a successful marriage!

Part III

The Right Kind of Love

The Perfect Relationship

9

Chapter Nine

The Perfect Relationship

f you are reading this chapter hoping to find out that you and your mate have the perfect relationship, or wanting to find the way to a perfect relationship in three easy steps, you are going to be disappointed. There is no such thing as a perfect relationship. It doesn't exist. However, what does exist is a perfect God, willing and able to guide and help us toward the most perfect love available to us here on earth.

If we are to consider ourselves committed Christians, then we cannot justifiably exclude the Lord from any area of our lives. This includes the one area in which we have a strong tendency to exclude Him because it is an exclusive situation—marriage, the most intimate relationship we can have with another person. However, we must not exclude our Creator from His creation. After all, He designed every one of us with the unique combination of ingredients that make us who we are and that cause others to find us attractive and compatible.

If it were not for our Creator, none of us would stand a chance at the wonderful experience of romance!

And He answered and said to them, "Have you not read that He who made them at the beginning 'made them male and female,' and said, 'For this reason a man shall leave his father and mother and be joined to his wife, and the two shall become one flesh'? So then, they are no longer two but one flesh. Therefore what God has joined together, let not man separate."
(Matthew 19:4–6)

If it were not for our Creator, none of us would stand a chance at the wonderful experience of romance! Our Lord reserves the right, therefore, to be an intimate partner in our personal and marital relationships.

For the husband is head of the wife, as also Christ is head of the church; and He is the Savior of the body.... For we are members of His body, of His flesh and of His bones. (Ephesians 5:23, 30)

God Himself wrote the textbook on love and marriage. First of all, God is the Author of love because it is His essential nature. True love originates in Him and flows from Him to us.

And we have known and believed the love that God has for us. God is love, and he who abides in love abides in God, and God in him. (1 John 4:16)

We love, because He first loved us. (1 John 4:19 NAS)

Second, relationships between the sexes and the rules of matrimony are clearly defined and elaborated upon throughout the richly layered text of the greatest book and most delectable romance novel ever written—the Bible. It makes perfect spiritual sense, then, that those of us who are romantically involved and espoused would have as the Head of our relationships the World's Greatest Lover as well as *"the author and finisher of our faith"* (Hebrews 12:2) and of our earthly alliances.

The Seasons of Intimate Relationships

When God is holding the reins and directing the individual paths of our lives, He also governs the relationships in which we have become *"one flesh"* with another. His control gives us a great assurance that we are abiding in His will and that our unions are pleasing to Him. Only with God's guidance will our relationships be certain to last and to be sustained through the cold, rough, inclement winters of romance, even as they flourish and are renewed during the enchanting spring times.

I opened for my beloved, but my beloved had turned away and was gone. My heart leaped up when he spoke. I sought him, but I could not find him; I called him, but he gave me no answer....I charge you, O daughters of Jerusalem, if you find my beloved, that you tell him I am lovesick! (Song of Solomon 5:6, 8)

These dry seasons of intimate relationships are inevitable. They come with the territory as we take up permanent residence in the lives of other individuals. The stormy times are part of the process of getting to know others for who they are. As we see them at their best and at their worst, they simultaneously come to know us in the same way. We all need to learn how to weather the worst and delight in the best.

We cannot get around the fact that our relationships require our time, patience, humble submission, faith in future possibilities, regular divine intervention, and our resolve to persevere.

Here on earth, there are no perfect relationships. This does not mean, however, that we have an excuse not to work on our unions tirelessly. Marriage does have the potential to become fabulously fulfilling, if we truly invest the commitment and dedication that we promised to have until the very end, when we first said our vows and became legally joined together.

The Importance of Commitment

One of the most essential ingredients in a successful marriage is commitment. When we were unattached and dating, ours was the luxury of getting to know different individuals. We could determine what we preferred in a mate and a relationship through our dating experiences.

When a relationship hit a dry period, when things were no longer going smoothly or accommodating our preferences, or when we generally lost interest, we could easily dispose of our partners (or be disposed of), essentially because no real commitment existed.

However, in dealing with our spouses, the individuals to whom we have vowed lifetime loyalty and fidelity, we must not cast them aside when it seems there is more discord than harmony in the household. This is not an option and should not even be considered. The strength of our commitment when we do not feel loving or loved is perhaps the best measure of the depth of our real love.

We cannot get around the fact that our relationships require our time, patience, humble submission, faith in future possibilities, regular divine intervention, and our resolve to persevere. When we were single, many of us prayed for the perfect mate and relationship, but somehow we expected it to come about without any serious exertion or struggle on our parts. Too many of us, it seems, are simply too apathetic to put in the necessary work a committed, intimate relationship requires.

It's Worth the Effort

At the time of this writing, my wife and I have been married for twenty-one years and are most definitely involved in a fabulous relationship with one another. Our marriage has not always been easy. In the beginning, primarily due to the lack of adequate finances to support and sustain our rapidly expanding household—we brought two children into the world within eleven months of each other—my wife and

I were at odds with one another. Whether we choose to admit it or not, money often has a lot to do with how smoothly a relationship functions.

At the same time, both of us had neglected our individual connections with God. This was probably more of a contributing factor to the initial difficulties we experienced than even our lack of finances was. Speaking for myself, I was also at a point in my career as an evangelist where I was more involved in the work of God than in His actual will for my life. This served as a major hindrance to the time I spent with my wife. Now that we have both grown considerably in grace and in unity with God's will, we have become much more in tune with each other, and we are both devoted to helping others achieve health and wholeness in their relationships.

I am now able to fully love my wife and support her as she leads a focused, fulfilled, and balanced life. God has taught me to understand her deeply. I see and appreciate the sheer essence of her femininity through simply observing her as she goes about her daily activities, from nurturing our children to keeping our household in order. With all she accomplishes, I am constantly amazed that she is still able to offer me such softly spoken words of comfort and wisdom in my times of distress.

Additionally, we work hard at keeping the lines of communication open. Instead of trying to figure out what pleases each other, we ask. Of course, we do not always see eye to eye on everything even now. Still, we have learned the art of good loving. We understand that it is about giving and taking, about sowing and reaping. We have learned that, ultimately, what you get out of a relationship is directly related to what you have put into it.

> *Do not be deceived, God is not mocked; for whatever a man sows, that he will also reap.* (Galatians 6:7)

Distinct Marital Personalities

Although marriage with all of its dynamics does not always live up to our personal ideal, it usually includes many rewards along with the sacrifices. The process of development and growth through conflict and resolution allows each particular marriage to shape and define itself. We must realize that no two marriages are alike. Through conciliation and passionate resolve, the bond of holy matrimony is strengthened and sealed; the lives of two separate individuals become one as instituted in the Word of God:

> *"For this reason a man shall leave his father and mother and be joined to his wife, and the two shall become one flesh." So then, they are no longer two but one flesh.* (Matthew 19:5–6)

Therefore, no two marriages should be patterned after each other. God has designed each marriage with its own set of fingerprints and personality, which distinguish it from any other marriage union. Thus, much of the advice we hear about how we ought to operate and function with our partners must be taken selectively. What I share is born out of my own personal experience and is what has worked for me and mine as we have tried to apply godly principles to our particular relationship.

A Third-Party Bond

Like us, every couple needs the divine guidance of the Holy Spirit in confronting and finding solutions to the problem areas of marriage. Most importantly, we all must seek God for ourselves and apply sound biblical principles to our marriages so that they may be prosperous as well as fulfilling for both partners. *"In all your ways acknowledge Him, and He shall direct your paths"* (Proverbs 3:6). As believers, we need the intimate involvement of that Third Person in our marital relationships if we are to love and abide with one another peacefully and successfully.

God is the only Third Party who should ever be allowed in a natural marriage relationship. When He is in the midst, the union is made complete.

However, God is the only Third Party who should ever be allowed in a natural marriage relationship. When He is in the midst, the union is made complete. This means that when coupled individuals first know God for themselves and then proceed to seek the Lord's guidance throughout the development of their relationship, He becomes the glue that binds them together through the good times and the bad, making what was a twofold union become a bonding together of three-in-one. As such, marriage becomes a reflection of the Godhead.

> *Two are better than one, because they have a good reward for their labor....Though one may be overpowered*

*by another, two can withstand him. And a threefold cord
is not quickly broken.*   (Ecclesiastes 4:9, 12)

Yes, there is strength in the bond between a couple, but the real source of power lies in the covenant that is formed when Christ is in the center of a relationship.

By Twos and by Threes

A beautician in my congregation likes to think of a hairstyling process that is most familiar to her, both in her profession and as the mother of four daughters, that vividly illustrates this Scripture concerning the relative strength in numbers. According to her, the braid, which is defined as "three or more strands of hair that are interwoven, interlaced, or entwined together," deftly represents *"a threefold cord."*

When her daughters were very little, one of the ways she styled their hair was by twisting, which involves taking two bunches of hair, wrapping them around one another, and then knotting them at the end. She says that this was a very pretty way of styling the hair, a style that her daughters preferred, in fact. However, it was also very inconvenient, because the twisted hair would unwind itself, and the hairstyle would come undone in just a few short hours. Twisting, then, became reserved for special occasions, when outward appearance was more important than durability and manageability.

Braiding, on the other hand, was the styling method she applied on a daily basis with her daughters. Unlike twisting, which requires two strands of hair, the braiding process calls for three. According to the beautician, this threefold interweaving of the hair sections was a much longer-lasting solution to the problem of tangled, messy hair! Braiding or plaiting the hair may take a much greater initial investment of time and energy than does twisting, but the dividends are well worth all of the work involved.

Furthermore, she notes that once some hair has been styled into a braid, there is no way to tell the three strands apart or to distinguish were one begins and the other ends. It is also impossible to separate or isolate one of the sections of hair from the other two without destroying the entire braid.

Likewise, so it is when we and our significant others have become one with each other and, simultaneously, with our Creator. We become intertwined, unable to tell one part from another, in something beautiful and stable. We become one.

United in Love

At the end of His earthly ministry, our Lord prayed this prayer for His disciples then and for us who would follow:

I do not pray for these alone, but also for those who will believe in Me through their word; that they all may be one, as You, Father, are in Me, and I in You; that they also may be one in Us, that the world may believe that You sent Me. And the glory which You gave Me I have given them, that they may be one just as We are one: I in them, and You in Me; that they may be made perfect in one, and that the world may know that You have sent Me, and have loved them as You have loved Me.
(John 17:20–23)

May you experience the ecstasy of unity with God and with your special loved ones, and may the Lord restore your relationships to the peak of their fulfillment.

About the Author

Bishop George G. Bloomer is a native of Brooklyn, New York. After serving as an evangelist for fourteen years, Bloomer began pastoring in 1996. He is the founder and senior pastor of Bethel Family Worship Center in Durham, North Carolina, but continues to travel extensively, sharing with others his testimony of how the Lord delivered him from a life of poverty, drug abuse, sexual abuse, and mental anguish. "God had a plan for my life," Bloomer now says, "and even during my span of lawlessness, the angels of the Lord were protecting me because the call of God was upon my life."

Bloomer holds a religious arts degree in Christian psychology and conducts many seminars dealing with relationships, finances, and stress management. He is founder of Young Witnesses for Christ, a youth evangelistic outreach ministry with several chapters on college campuses throughout the United States, and bishop of C.L.U.R.T (Come Let Us Reason Together) International Assemblies, comprised of over eighty churches nationwide and abroad. His message is one of deliverance and of a hope that far exceeds the desperation and oppression of many silent sufferers.

She's not the same woman you married. He's not the man you thought he was. Sometimes in a marriage relationship, things can get crazy and out of control. The decisions made in those times determine the strength of the household you build. You can begin to reconstruct the building blocks that will put sanity and stability into the foundation of your relationship. Discover the keys to building a strong house, a strong marriage, and a strong future. Crazy house or sane house—the choice is yours!

Crazy House, Sane House
George and Jeannie Bloomer
ISBN: 0-88368-726-7 • Trade • 144 pages

Empowered from Above
George G. Bloomer
ISBN: 0-88368-285-0 • Trade • 160 pages

Are you walking in power as Christ did? Is your desire for intimacy with the Father increasing? Prepare to discover a deeper understanding of the indwelling of the Holy Spirit. Don't be lost in this doctrinal tug-of-war. Join Bishop George G. Bloomer as he provides solid, scriptural answers on the Holy Spirit—His person, His fruits, His gifts, His unifying work. There's no need to live in confusion any longer. As you begin to walk in this deeper understanding, you will be filled with new wisdom, power, and strength. Prepare to be *Empowered from Above.*

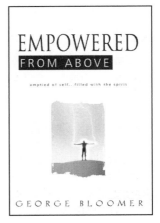

WHITAKER HOUSE

proclaiming the power of the Gospel through the written word
visit our website at www.whitakerhouse.com

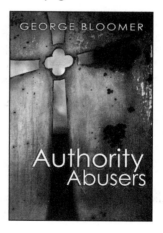

Spiritual Authority Series (5 CD Set)

George G. Bloomer

Authority—at its best, it's a blessing, a representation of the Lord's gracious guidance and leading of His sheep. However, when tainted by sin and selfishness, authority can turn into a curse. It doesn't matter where this authority comes into play—the classroom, the church, the home, or the workplace. What matters is that God-given authority is in alignment with the Lord's perfect provision for leadership. In this dynamic series, Bishop George Bloomer explores principles that can ensure the proper exercise of authority in every area of our lives.

ISBN: 0-88368-966-9 • 5 CDs • UPC: 6-30809-68966-5
(The CDs in this set are also available individually.)

Anointed for an Appointed Time
ISBN: 0-88368-967-7 • CD • UPC: 6-30809-68967-2

Departing Spirits
ISBN: 0-88368-969-3 • CD • UPC: 6-30809-68969-6

Everyone Needs a Friend, Friend
ISBN: 0-88368-968-5 • CD • UPC: 6-30809-68968-9

Witchcraft in the Pews
ISBN: 0-88368-970-7 • CD • UPC: 6-30809-68970-2

Witchcraft in the Pulpit
ISBN: 0-88368-971-5 • CD • UPC: 6-30809-68971-9

WHITAKER HOUSE

www.whitakerhouse.com